DOMESTIC RELIGION

Work, Food, Sex, and Other Commitments

FOREWORD BY PHYLLIS TICKLE

THE PILGRIM PRESS

CLEVELAND, OHIO

To Annette and
Milton Greenhouse,
with love and gratitude.

The Pilgrim Press, Cleveland, Ohio 44115
© 1998 by Peter Gardella

Biblical quotations are from the New Revised Standard Version of the Bible,
© 1989 by the Division of Christian Education of the National Council of the
Churches of Christ in the U.S.A., and are used by permission

Printed in the United States of America on acid-free paper

03   02   01   00   99   98   5   4   3   2   1

Library of Congress Cataloging-in-Publication Data

Gardella, Peter, 1951–
     Domestic religion : work, food, sex, and other commitments / Peter Gardella.
        p.   cm.
     Includes bibliographical references.
     ISBN 0-8298-1277-6 (pbk. : alk. paper)
        1. United States—Religious life and customs.   2. Religious life.   I. Title.
     BL2525.G37   1998
     200'.973—dc21   98-21722
                                                                                      CIP

CONTENTS

FOREWORD

There's a rather antique but instructive story that jumps into my head every time I read sociological analyses of the present state of American religion. It was told to me by a clergy friend who did his seminary work when hospital and clinical counseling courses involved onsite psychiatric observation preceded by lectures. In my friend's case the lectures were by a crusty old German, who began every session saying, "Now, Gentlemen, I am about to describe for you the elephant in the room."

"And he was right every time," my friend chuckles. "That brusque old German never told us anything we didn't already know, but he told us everything we hadn't seen about what we knew. It was amazing."

If the image of an undescribed elephant in the room was valid as a metaphor for psychiatric lectures forty years ago, it is ten times over more applicable nowadays to those like Peter Gardella and me who are mesmerized by the sociology of American religion. America is in the midst of a religious foment that in its agitation, ubiquity, and intensity bears an unsettling resemblance to the Protestant Reformation as well as to the Great Awakening. Neither of those prior tumults happened, however, in a culture or time that was media-intensive, chronically mobile, or consumer oriented. For the first time since Christianity's opening decades, religious reformation is being sculpted not by an ecclesial institution, but by the popular culture. The old unity that once we referred to simply as "religion" has now splintered into a multitude of subsets. And into that mix now comes yet another division and yet another term, "domestic religion," with which to name it.

Peter Gardella's thesis is that below all the doctrine, creeds, and organizations there is, and always has been, a religion composed of humanity's daily choices. Using this thesis, Gardella persuasively argues that, whereas such substructure did not previously impinge either on formal religion's statement of itself or upon public beliefs and practices outside its own immediate locale, this is no longer the case. Rather, as Gardella shows us, in a society homogenized by media and mass communications, what used to be simply a "domestic" set of values and beliefs has now seeped out to become an agency in the culture at large and to have arrived at such unity and volume as to effect doctrinal religion itself.

There is, beyond any doubt, an elephant in the room. Professor Gardella didn't make that elephant or even invite him into our room; nor by describing the elephant does Professor Gardella really tell us much that we haven't been more or less aware of all along. What he does do, like my clergyman's German mentor, is expose to us the significance and implications—the truth, if you will—of just what it is that we have been so innocently aware of. His is, additionally, the first sketch, so far as I know, of this particular part of the big elephant's anatomy; and that fact alone would make this book worthy of our attention.

PHYLLIS TICKLE

FROM RELIGION TO DOMESTIC RELIGION

Ask people what they mean by religion and they usually mention God, rules for moral behavior, and whatever happens in their churches, synagogues, or temples. But behind those beliefs, codes, and forms of worship lie the rituals and values they live by at home: the holiday things that absolutely have to be done; the kinds of success for which no sacrifice or effort would be too much; the sports events that connect with the whole struggle of life; the songs that stand for transcendent love, sadness, and joy; the television shows that express exactly how life is, or should be; and the foods and drinks that can yield the last happiness of old age. This is the realm of domestic religion.

According to one of the first analysts of religion, the ancient Roman poet Lucretius, the word *religion* combines the prefix for "repetition" with the Latin word *ligare,* "to bind" (as in ligament).[1] A *religion* is a system of nonrational commitments that hold life together. Formal or traditional religions like Christianity, Judaism, and Islam are described in many books. This book explores various informal systems and how those systems work together.

A *religion* is a system of nonrational commitments that hold life together.

Not everyone has a religion. Just as some people love no music, others have no deep commitments. A few try to live rationally, calculating the costs and benefits of their commitments according to some philosophy. For most people, however, the power of certain ideas, words, names, places, actions, symbols, and stories gives shape to the world. Not necessarily without reason or against reason, but before reason (*nonrational*), some commitments seem worthy of respect that extends to sacrifice. Some objects and gestures can do more than console in the face of death. As William James observed a century ago, philosophy may help people sustain courage in the face of suffering, but only religion can make people happier even as they suffer.[2]

Religious behavior often appears in ordinary circumstances, accompanied by little or no awareness. Every day, not only in churches and temples but also in homes and offices, gymnasiums and restaurants, people live according to nonrational systems of values, rituals, symbols, and myths. Some rituals, such as the Muslim noon prayer, relate directly to formal world religions that have goals transcending daily life. Other commitments, such as the moral obligations that millions feel to brush their teeth, to exercise, and to pursue success in their careers, may have no transcendent goals but hold life together now.

Yet domestic religion, even though privately practiced, connects with traditional religions and resonates with the public culture. As the means of communication proliferate and research into behavior grows more sophisticated, many people consult not only with friends and family but also with distant experts and professionals—manufacturers and advertisers, doctors and journalists, clergy and teachers—regarding how to eat, how much to value sex, what attitudes to take toward work and success, and how to celebrate the winter solstice, among other things.

Take food as an example. Many religions regulate food, with standards ranging from the kosher laws of Judaism to the Muslim fast of Ramadan to the Jain abstinence from killing plants. But in any restaurant in the United States, and to some extent in England or Germany, another set of rules comes into play, establishing new categories of righteousness and sin. Any group of middle-aged and middle-class diners is likely to include a vegetarian who abstains from eating animals on ethical or spiritual grounds that arise from no formal religion at all. Yet this commitment is routinely understood by the others at the table (and by those in the restaurant business, who increasingly provide vegetarian choices). And anyone who orders veal will probably feel the need to apologize or defend that choice.

Almost every adult in the group will be counting calories; those who also limit the fat and salt content of their food will have a moral edge. The menu may describe desserts as "sinful." Even if the rhetoric of taboo is absent, the atmosphere of dalliance with sin will play around the table when the dessert cart arrives, or when the server recites the dessert options. Meals have traditionally involved religious blessings, but in the domestic religion of the United States many foods also entail curses and temptations.

The diners face another thicket of issues surrounding alcohol and tobacco. Someone at the table may well be in recovery from addiction; someone else may have signed on to be a designated driver. Once, smoking before and after dinner was routine, but now anyone who smokes is certain to give moral offense to a nonsmoker.

Dinner conversation will reveal more aspects of domestic religion. If the group discusses sports, sensational crimes such as rape, assault, or illegal drug use may come up, as well as controversies over municipal subsidies for stadiums and the wealth and lack of public spirit of players and owners. Beneath the surface of such momentary topics runs a river of discourse that began a century ago, regarding the spiritual aspect of a fan's commitment to specific sports, teams, and athletes. What kind of person follows baseball or football, women's basketball or professional soccer, tennis or golf? Talk may extend beyond the day's game into history, aesthetics, and morality, suggesting the mythic meanings of what athletes, coaches, and owners accomplish on and off the field.

All dinner conversation, and indeed all life in the United States for nearly three months between Halloween and Super Bowl Sunday, falls into the shadow of an enormous mid-

Domestic religion, even though privately practiced, connects with traditional religions and resonates with the public culture.

A shift from sacred

time to secular begins

with the descent into

symbolic chaos.

winter holiday, the center of which extends from Thanksgiving to Christmas. Unifying pagan, Christian, Jewish, and civil-religious elements, this season also gains power from its position in the school year and in the tax code. A shift from sacred time to secular begins with the descent into symbolic chaos, when the parties reach midnight and the ball drops above Times Square on December 31; but business does not completely resume until after the Super Bowl.

If our hypothetical group talk about what they have seen on television, they enter a jungle of religious flora and fauna. Weekly comedies, dramas, and daily talk shows consider ever more closely intense controversies in morality and religion. What does the audience say to the man who cheated with his wife's mother? How should Christians and Jews handle intermarriage? The sister of the most conservative House Speaker in sixty years has appeared on television as a lesbian minister performing a wedding for two women who are regulars on a popular sitcom. Played out in comedy and drama and talked out by audiences and hosts, the standards for acceptable behavior in the United States undergo constant changes and tests.

Those changes affect every nation in the developed world. Every culture has a moral discourse, and every country has a domestic religion. In the United States, however, the relative weakness of family and church traditions makes the common and commercial elements of domestic religion more obvious. The position of the United States in the world economy also means that U.S. heroes, fashions, and moral issues are quickly exported. People all over the world find that their own cultures must confront nonrational commitments that people in the United States have come to see as natural.

The U.S. civil religion—the complex of symbols, holidays, and values to which all citizens of the country are called to subscribe, alongside their commitments to traditional religions—was compellingly described by sociologist Robert Bellah in 1967. In 1986 historian Colleen McDannell identified a domestic religion in the Victorian homes that were linked by the first mass markets of the industrial age. In her later books, *Heaven: A History* and *Material Christianity*, McDannell has explored aspects of domestic religion in gratifying detail, but without moving the discussion beyond its Christian and nineteenth-century roots into the current, interdenominational and interreligious world. Another group of scholars, including Robert Orsi, Leigh Eric Schmidt, Nancy Ammerman, and David D. Hall, have advanced the concept of "lived religion" to study practice rather than belief; but their work so far has focused on particular practices and groups rather than the ordinary, everyday practices of the entire culture.[3]

Both Bellah and McDannell take inspiration from Emile Durkheim, a French social theorist who wrote that any society unified in its economic life would also have a unified religious system, a collective conscience that teaches individuals what ideals they should affirm. In the United States, what Durkheim would predict has taken place: the denominational differences that Protestants fought over for centuries have lost all their importance, while the divisions of Protestants and Catholics and Christians and Jews have also blurred. Alan Wolfe's 1998 study *One Nation, After All* found broad tolerance for different religions even in conservative cities in Oklahoma and Georgia. The 1990s have seen Muslims, Hindus, Buddhists, Native American traditionalists, and many other groups—as Diana Eck reports in several articles—entering the U.S. mainstream with remarkable rapidity. Ideas such as yoga breathing, reincarnation, ancestor worship, and the power of *chi,* once the exotic fare of world religion courses, now affect the lives of ordinary people through a classmate at school or a course at the YMCA. Each society tends to have one religion.[4]

In bookstores, catechisms of domestic religion often appear in the shelves marked personal development and self-help rather than in the religion section. Spiritual teachers such as Thomas Moore, the former monk who wrote *Care of the Soul* and *The Re-Enchantment of Everyday Life,* and Kathleen Norris, author of *Dakota* and *The Cloister Walk,* line up here alongside health writers such as Bernie S. Siegel (*Faith, Love, and Healing*), and exercise gurus such as Mirka

In bookstores, catechisms of domestic religion often appear in the shelves marked personal development and self-help rather than in the religion section.

Different symbols

may lead people to the

same destination.

Knaster (*Discovering the Body's Wisdom*). One recent survey of the discourse about religion in U.S. culture, Phyllis Tickle's *God-Talk in America*, also sells in the personal development section of my local Barnes and Noble, and my book may land there too. Unlike most authors in personal development, however, my interest lies less in directly telling people how to live than in helping all of us, myself included, by deciphering and describing how the domestic religion works, so that we can better cope with the rituals, values, and commitments that surround us every day.

The cultural distances between groups in the United States, compounded by racism and economic inequality, mean that its domestic religion has a distinctly pluralistic character. The government builds monuments, declares holidays, and legislates pledges of allegiance and national anthems, and so assures that the civil religion remains unified. The media conglomerates that profit from nonrational commitments, however, have less interest in visible unity. In the same home, some may participate in the religion of sports and others in a cult within the religion of entertainment, such as the cults formed by fans of *Star Wars* or by the following of a musician. Another person may have nonrational commitments in the realm of food, exercise, sex, or all three. As long as these divisions of the domestic religion remain compatible on basic issues, such as the importance of the material world and attitudes toward work and success, their separate practices ultimately reinforce each other.

Different symbols may lead people to the same destination, as when Hindus choose to sit in meditation or to dance, and among gods to pay homage to Nandi, the bull of Shiva, or to Mother Kali, or to Ganesha the elephant-god. For Hindus, these varieties of devotion serve individual deliverance, and it may be that the personal commitments of U.S. citizens serve equally individual goals. Emile Durkheim feared that the division of labor in modern societies would result in a collective conscience without social content. Writing more than a century ago, Durkheim described a continual weakening of social obligations and growth of individualism throughout history, a process that undermined all religions except for "a cult in behalf of personal dignity which . . . already has its superstitions." Although the collective conscience of modern societies was "common in so far as the community partakes of it, it is individual in its object," he complained; even though the modern collective conscience "turns all wills toward the same end, this end is not social."[5]

As a sociologist, Durkheim may not have appreciated the psychological and biological depths at which religions connect people. Below the surfaces of social and cultural life, religions also touch and draw power from the unsearchable depths of human nature that have been suggested by scholars such as Joseph Campbell, Carl Jung, Mircea Eliade, and Rudolf Otto.[6] Rhythms of sex and the seasons, death and rebirth; readiness for the emotional conflicts of families; and responses to natural phenomena such as the sea and the womb, mountains and storms, the sun and the moon, seem likely to have become programmed into the nervous system of a species that evolved over billions of years on this earth.

Religions do claim to represent Truth, obtained through intuition or inspiration, but the claim of revelation or absolute Truth will always be (by definition) untestable. Whether or not religions have access to Truth, on the human side successful religions function according to laws of behavioral psychology, as systems of rewards and punishments, stimuli and reinforcements more effective and sophisticated than any behaviorist could invent and enforce. The world religions that flourish in the United States today and that contribute to the domestic religion have perpetuated themselves by producing reliable effects among hundreds of millions of people and adapting, while helping their followers to adapt, to changing conditions for thousands of years.

The last meeting of religions on such even ground (though not on this scale) took place in ancient Rome, where Lucretius and Cicero became the first Western thinkers to speculate about religion in general. Out of the religious syncretism and competition of the Roman Empire came Christianity; and alongside the Christian creeds and churches grew new norms for sexual relations, child care, economic behavior, sports, entertainment, and every other aspect of daily life.[7]

We cannot tell whether any new world religion will emerge in our day. Most evangelical Christians and some conservative Catholics and Jews fear a conspiracy of New Age believ-

We cannot tell whether any new world religion will emerge in our day.

ers. Yet the age of Aquarius has so far demonstrated little organizational force. On the domestic side, however, transformations of values that took centuries in the ancient world now occur in decades. Through modern communications media, powered by the relentless drive of international business, certain ideals of success and of health, particular holidays and a particular rhythm of the year, new rules for sexual relations and new demigods of sports and entertainment can emerge overnight and develop instant followings in the United States and around the world.

This book will describe aspects of the domestic religion—the systematic and coherent sets of nonrational commitments, expressed in explicit rituals and values, regarding the facts of daily life—that now command the broadest consensus. Although focusing on the United States, the analysis will include ancient and international currents of religious thought and practice, both because these currents flow through the United States and because the heritage of world religions offers perspectives that show what is distinctive about the contemporary situation. Without advocating any particular religion, but guided by my own nonrational commitments, some of the chapters will suggest alternative approaches when modern Americans seem, from my standpoint as a historian of religions, to be headed for dead ends of development.

Because the world's religions embody proven wisdom, it may hold practical as well as academic interest to consider the rituals and values of everyday life in the light of religious traditions. The wisdom of religion does not always coincide with faith, love, awareness, or compassion, however, and the conclusion of the book must take up the question of whether people might be better off without domestic religions, or even without religions of any kind.

SUCCESS   · 2 ·

Driven by the need for success, I sit down to write. Money could not lead me to work this hard, to think this intensely, or to commit myself this completely unless I were desperate; but success drives even those who have enough money.

Success means what salvation once meant. Millions who practice no organized religion (and millions who do) call themselves to regular internal judgments on the basis of their standards for success. Have they done well in school, in their careers, in their families? Have they made good use of their opportunities and their gifts? To conclude that one has succeeded in life offers the only consolation in facing death that many will accept.

Success represents the most common moral commitment in the contemporary United States. In admissions essays for college, millions of students describe their commitment to success as the sacred value that the admissions committee should recognize, the value to which the students assume the college is committed as well. Although we want wealth for what it can buy, we value wealth more as a sign of success, a way to keep score. We fear poverty for good, material reasons, particularly in a culture that offers no rights to food or shelter, but we fear poverty first as a sign of failure.

Success means what salvation once meant. Even those without careers see life in terms of success. Having children and successfully raising them, particularly for women but also for men, is a common standard by which we judge our success or failure. Making a difference in our communities, through the parent-teacher association or the church or in politics, can help us to feel that we have succeeded. A great deal of the appeal of sports and exercise for those who participate in them—and also for those who watch—derives from the need for success.

One weakness of success as a value appears in the word itself. *Success* derives from the Latin for "follow," as in the word *successor* or the line of hereditary *succession* to a throne or a title. In this sense, only one person can succeed at a time. One person's success often means another's failure, or the failure of many. Envy and negative judgments of others attach naturally to the value of success. As a bitter old saying goes, "It isn't enough that I succeed; all my friends must also fail." And of course, success is temporary. Succession in the root sense of the word would begin at a definite point, with the replacement of a predecessor, and end at one's own death or deposition. In the modern sense, success can begin and end again and again.

Let me illustrate the radically temporary nature of success with my own life. At forty-six, I hold a tenured position teaching religion at a small college. While making less money than a police officer in New York (or a rookie police officer in several less dangerous cities in the suburbs), I do work that I love, and I have more control of my time than most people do. I published one book, thirteen years ago, with more success than usual in academics, although the book brought the failure of a crucial bad review in the *New York Times*. My wife also has a tenured position, at another small college; she and I have stayed together sixteen years, and we have one child; the three of us live in a heavily mortgaged house that we bought five years ago. If I could have seen myself thirty years ago in this house, with this woman and these diplomas and other accomplishments, I would have been not simply happy but ecstatic. Seen from outside, my life offers a picture of stable good fortune, health and wealth, and happiness.

But lived from inside, moments of breathtaking success have temporarily dispelled a continual fear of failure. Success has brought thrills: I have won races at track meets in high school and finished road races as an adult; received acceptance letters and fellowships from Harvard and Yale; walked out of a publisher's office with a check for ten thousand dollars.

On the other hand, I recall working on my first book in the uniform of a Pinkerton security guard, an outfit that made me feel like a failure from the first moment that I wore it (and noticed that my predecessor had left half a marijuana joint in the pants pocket). In constant financial stress, no doubt due to my mismanagement, I consider taking up guarding on weekends again. These last few years have been plagued with worry over the struggles of small colleges to survive and flourish; my attempts to deal with these worries have led to several public failures in campus politics. For example, two years ago I was reviewed for promotion from the rank of associate to full professor, and the president and provost of the college turned me down.

The bad review of my book showed me the intimate link between success and failure. Imagine how it must feel for those involved with a Broadway show or a movie, a new model of car, or any new business—enterprises that represent a great success, simply to have brought them out in public—to be rejected, to see the business fail a month after it opened, the play get a bad review and close in a week. Such experiences can color the most successful lives with failure.

Undermining my own sense of success is my judgment that I have not written enough. Accomplishments in teaching or curriculum reform or faculty organization satisfy some of the need for success, but they leave no lasting result that compares to a book or even an article. If I do not write at least one or two books that succeed as well as my first (and ideally, a little better), I will see my academic career as a failure. My sense of failure connects with a foolish, needless envy that poisons some relationships, particularly with colleagues at other institutions who have published more, who have been promoted, whose names are better known in the national organization. But the authentic depth of my need to write comes from the conviction that if I do not, I will have wasted a talent for which I should be held accountable.

Surely this last conviction deserves the name of a religious commitment. But the question remains whether I, or anyone, ought to think of life this way. The world's religious

One person's success often means another's failure.

> Failure connects
>
> with a foolish, needless
>
> envy that poisons some
>
> relationships.

traditions offer some affirmations of the value of success, some warnings against taking success too seriously, and some wisdom regarding why we take success so seriously in this culture. The Christian Scriptures often connect salvation to the drive to succeed. According to the parable of the talents, recorded in Matthew 25:14–30 and in another version in Luke 19, Jesus taught the nature of the dominion of God with the story of a rich man who went on a journey and left his servants in charge of his fortune. To the first servant he gave five talents of silver, an amount worth about seventy-five years of the wages of a laborer; to the second he gave two talents, or about thirty years' wages; and to the third he gave one talent, about fifteen years' wages.[1] When the man came back, his first servant reported that he could return the five talents with the addition of five more; the second had also doubled his two talents; but the third, fearing the wrath of his master, had hidden his talent in the ground, and now returned it without increase. "Take the talent from him, and give it to the one with the ten talents," the master said. He dismissed his fearful and unfruitful servant, instructing others to "throw him into the outer darkness, where there will be weeping and gnashing of teeth."

Before any of the Gospels were written, Paul's letter to the Christians in the Greek city of Corinth used their familiarity with athletic contests to urge them to keep their appetites for sex, food, and drink in check, and so to succeed in Christian life. "Do you not know that in a race the runners all compete, but only one receives the prize? Run in such a way that you may win it. Athletes exercise self-control in all things; they do it to receive a perishable wreath, but we an imperishable one" (1 Cor. 9:24–25).

This ethic of success belongs in the Christian Scriptures because the Christian movement arose in a world of individuals, a world where nations and religions and families were dissolving in the universal culture of Rome. But most religions use fewer images of athletes and investors. In fact, most religions have little need for any concept of individual success. In Jewish tradition, for example, salvation is collective. The Torah says nothing about eternal life and essentially does not address individuals; the Ten Commandments, for example, are given to the whole people whom God has led out of Egypt. The 613 laws of the Torah do not propose to bring people to salvation or help them succeed, but to form a special people to testify for God before the other nations of the world. Later, the prophets began to think about judgment and the end of the world, and in such visions as Ezekiel 37–38 and Daniel 12 hope emerged for the resurrection of the dead—all the dead, some raised to glory and some to disgrace—on the last day, or in the days of the Messiah. But even in these visions of judgment, Jewish prophecies focused on the whole people of Israel and their relations with God and with the other peoples of the world.

To move from Jewish to early Christian writings is to enter a more selfish atmosphere. The disciples argue about who will be first, who will sit on the right hand of the Messiah. Individuals come to Jesus asking what they must do to be saved. Believers are warned not to grow weary, not to let their lamps go out, not to be caught without appropriate clothing—not to fail. By contrast, individuals in the Hebrew Scriptures do cry out to God in prayer, but always for deliverance from a particular enemy or a physical threat, never for eternal life. Prophets and teachers of wisdom urge ancient Israel to work hard and to avoid vices like adultery and drunkenness as a practical matter, not because the Israelites stand in danger that their lives will end in failure.

The death of Jesus in failure and despair, as the crucifixion is described in Mark and Matthew, undercuts the Christian emphasis on success and at the same time confirms it. Alone, his followers having fled, Jesus asks why God has forsaken him; he seems to have no sense of his own salvation, much less the success of his proclamation of God's dominion. The power of the gospel lives in this story, because anyone may die in despair, abandoned and without any sense of God's love. Mark tells us that Jesus died in this way but was raised from the dead. If we lose our life, we will gain it, as the antithetical aphorisms quoted from Jesus teach; those who are last will be first, and those who would lead should be the servants of all. Christians should aim to succeed by keeping faith in the midst of failure. According to the doctrine of original sin and the expectations of Christian eschatology, the human race and the creation itself are both abject failures,

Most religions have little need for any concept of individual success.

Islam brings together the Jewish and Christian perspectives on success.

subject to sin and death and condemnation, but God rescues those who acknowledge their need.

Islam brings together the Jewish and Christian perspectives on success, as on many other questions. From the minaret, five times a day the muezzin urges people to hurry to prayer (*al-salat*) and to hurry to *al-falah*, which literally means "success," although it is sometimes translated "salvation" to convey its full meaning to Christian minds.[2] Muslim success includes everlasting life, as in Christianity, and each person must come to it through an individual judgment; but Islam teaches success through an attitude of submission or peace (Arabic *salaam,* the term related to the Hebrew *shalom,* from which Islam takes its name). Like Jews, Muslims regard themselves as capable of succeeding without first failing, but rather by doing what they should; like Christians, Muslims focus religious life on the individual attainment of paradise, rather than on the collective life of God's people.

Instead of the Christian valleys and peaks of sin, crucifixion, despair, and grace, Islam prescribes a straight path of belief, prayer, fasting, charity, and pilgrimage. Perhaps the Muslim concept of salvation through submission lends itself to an easier attitude toward worldly success, which has never become the compulsion in Muslim cultures that it has in Christian. Islam also has never had the problems of Christianity in handling riches; vows of poverty and guilt over having wealth are both alien to Islam. Neither beggars nor oil sheiks feel marked as religious or moral failures in Islam, so long as they answer the muezzin's call and come to prayer, to success.

But how easy it is for Christians to think that success indicates righteousness; for Jews to see success as a prerogative or a requirement of their historic mission; for Muslims to presume that the success they meet is one with the will of God to which they submit. The mind, as Martin Luther said, is a busy workshop making idols, and success can be one of the strongest.

Fortunately, religions can also teach how to let go of success. The first two noble truths of the Buddha—that all is suffering and that suffering stems from attachment—show how every success opens new chances for failure; every step upward raises the potential energy of the fall. How cunningly good things lead to more desire. To think in terms of success and failure will cause suffering in itself, increasing the delusion that the world divides between subject and object, winner and loser, and that some people could occupy only one side, when in fact all existing things are equally insubstantial, impermanent, and painful.[3]

In China, confronting Confucian ideals of success through respect for humanity, ritual, and history, the *Tao Te Ching* taught that if learning disappeared, so would ignorance, and that the end of the formal, gentlemanly behavior of Confucian leaders would greatly benefit the people. An ideal Taoist ruler, guiding the world through unity with the Way that runs through nature, doing nothing to interfere, could set all things in order without succeeding in any sense that the Western world would recognize.[4]

Perhaps we all succeed. The drunk succeeds at drinking, the butcher at butchering, the writer at writing. After these identities wear out, others replace them. The faces of today's desire succeed the faces of yesterday's. In the end—a judgment that happens constantly, because the faces have no substance, and (as the Muslims say) God is closer to us than we are to ourselves, or (as the Buddhists say) only awareness is entirely real—success comes as a gift, in the form exactly suited to whatever we prepare to receive.

The value of success in the 1990s has extended and generalized the "spirit of capitalism" that Max Weber, one of the first sociologists of religion, saw developing in the Reformation of the 1500s and described early in this century. What Weber called the Protestant ethic, a set of behaviors that included self-denial and reinvestment, entered common usage in the less critical and less threatening form of the Protestant *work* ethic.[5] Now, in the domestic religion of Americans, the most sacred commitment after success is the commitment to work.

3 ·

WORK

Work defines most of the hours of most of our days. When people are not working, they are getting ready for work or recovering from work, looking for work, trying to avoid work or worrying about work. In setting social policies and in planning our lives, modern people give the central place to work. Our arrangements for child care and education, our personal identities and hopes for material comfort, and our attitudes toward the economic system and the natural world all relate to the kinds of work we do. Every traditional religion includes values regarding work, but most of these values are out-of-date, leaving traces of archaic behavior that may keep our domestic religion from realizing its potential to hold our lives and our communities together today.

When people in the United States lament the loss of the work ethic or give speeches on the value of work, they probably have what has been called the "Protestant ethic" in mind. First named early in this century by pioneer sociologist Max Weber, the Protestant ethic has served to justify the winners of the capitalist lotteries of the West by showing that they worked harder, or at least more systematically. The Protestant ethic still leads many people in the United States to seek out their vocations with anxiety and to suspect those who have no productive work. But the heirs of Weber's hero, Ben Franklin, often fail to recognize the other ethics at work in this country today. These include a peasant ethic among some Catholics and Jews; a Jewish and Asian ethic of pariah capitalism; Confucian and Shinto ethics from China and Japan; an evangelical, charismatic ethic that may work for justice or call on the Holy Spirit to cover the world with Domino's Pizza and theme parks; and a complex ethic with roots in Africa and in slavery, shaped by a century of segregation.

Weber began the discussion of religion and work ethics by observing that the Protestant parts of Europe were wealthier and more oriented toward industry and trade, while Catholic countries were more agricultural and poorer.[1] The difference seemed especially significant in areas that were geographically and culturally close to each other but separated by religion, such as Germany and Austria or the cantons of Switzerland. According to Weber, these differences resulted from a Protestant revolution in thinking that changed the field of meaningful work from the sacred to the secular while shifting power from priests, kings, and aristocrats to the middle class.

Catholics have traditionally believed that they could reach heaven by many means, including going to Mass, obeying their priests, receiving the sacraments, buying the forgiveness of sins with indulgences, or in the last resort, by the intervention of the Virgin Mary and the saints. When Martin Luther and the Protestant movement preached that salvation came by faith alone, and that faith was a gift of God, they left a terrible anxiety in the hearts of their followers. One could do nothing to earn or to purchase salvation. How could one even know one had faith? Weber wrote that this gap of assurance was filled by work.

In the monasteries and convents, in the palaces of the nobility and the kings, the rulers of the Catholic world saw their rights challenged. They had organized the world as a hierarchy in which aristocrats had a duty not to work but to rule, and priests were obliged to perform ceremonies. Now Luther, Calvin, and the English Puritans taught that God had no use for human hierarchies and ceremonies. Only faith saved, and faith came from believing in the promises of the Bible. Those who had faith would work faithfully in their vocations—a word that comes from the same root as "vocal," and means the task to which God calls people. To preach the gospel was the work of a Christian minister or elder; all the other forms of prayer and works of charity

Every traditional religion includes values regarding work.

were useless, or worse than useless if they led people to trust in them as guarantees of salvation. A middle-class morality, setting its highest value on practical work in a trade or a profession, banished both aristocrats and monks from Protestant countries.

While Protestants recognized that work could not earn heaven any more than ceremonies could, at least work offered a negative assurance, that one was not surely lost—unlike the poor who did not work and therefore were certainly not saved. In the old system, believers were supposed to regard a beggar as an opportunity. St. Francis of Assisi taught that Franciscans should always beg, because those who gave to them would gain merit for themselves, while those who turned them down would help the brothers to grow in humility. In the middle of the 1990s, Mother Teresa still said that she served the poor because it was in the poor that she found Christ. But in the United States today, as in Protestant countries for the last five hundred years, the beggar reminds most people of the damned. We may not have complete confidence that our own work in our vocation represents the will of God, but we feel certain that God did not call the beggar to beg.

If we do not find a vocation, or if we do not work hard enough to succeed in one, we feel guilty. Meanwhile, all that hard work done to avoid guilt also brings monetary rewards; people who practice the Protestant ethic tend to grow rich. John Wesley, the founder of Methodism, noticed this process in the 1740s. But Jesus of Nazareth and his first followers were poor, as the Christian Scriptures frequently report. One reason why the monks and nuns proliferated in medieval Christendom was that people wanted a practical way to continue living in the poverty of the Christian Scriptures. Rich people seemed un-Christian by the standards of the Gospels and the Epistles. How could Protestants handle the riches their work generated without taking vows of poverty and returning to the monasteries which they had rejected in the name of salvation by faith?

The pattern of behavior that Weber called "worldly asceticism" kept Protestants from drowning their new faith in riches. Asceticism comes from the Greek word for exercise; it has been a word much loved by Christian moralists and spiritual advisors. All monks and nuns and members of religious orders are considered "ascetics." But the exercises of monks and nuns are directed away from this world; they sought their own salvation after death and the salvation of others through intercessory prayer. On the other hand, Protestant "worldly ascetics" disciplined their appetites by working for the sake of God's dominion on earth. Protestants worked and saved, not for a particular goal but as a way of life, denying themselves worldly comforts for the sake of their calling. When rational capitalism and Enlightenment thinking displaced the dream of God's dominion, working and saving remained as foundational values in the new world. Through worldly asceticism, the Protestant ethic became what Weber called "the spirit of capitalism."

To put it simply: people the world over have always wanted wealth or money, and some people have always been greedy. But most people spend money when they have it, and many will stop working when they have an amount of wealth they consider enough for their security, or to satisfy their physical desires. In a bazaar in the traditional cultures of the Mideast, the owner of a stall may close down and go home if he has made a very large profit on a sale; or to use an example from Weber, raising the rate that workers are paid for mowing sections of a field may cause them to stop work earlier, choosing to work less for the same money rather than to produce more.[2]

The person who works in the spirit of capitalism never has enough and feels too much responsibility to leave work early or to close his business on a whim. Impelled by the momentum of the Protestant ethic, believing (perhaps in some secular or therapeutic version) the doctrine that work is a calling from God and idleness a sign of damnation, the true capitalist would feel guilty after going home. Nor will the capitalist spend excess wealth on flashy vehicles, luxurious homes, and flamboyant clothing. The spirit of capitalism demands that people seem seriously committed to work, not leisure. If they spend on themselves, understated quality must be the rule; if they engage in recreation, it must be demanding of energy or justified by its benefits for health and for increasing the capacity for work. Recent history has offered the example of President George Bush supposedly relaxing on vacation in Maine—which meant rising at dawn to play golf, then fishing, then racing around in a cigarette boat and holding news conferences on the crisis in the Mideast. Another presi-

Aristocrats had a duty not to work but to rule.

Believers were supposed

to regard a beggar as an

opportunity.

dential ascetic, Jimmy Carter, once pushed himself so hard while jogging for "recreation" that he fainted.

Besides working hard, those who practice worldly asceticism also save money, which gives them a special role in the birth of capitalism as a system; but Americans notoriously no longer save. George Bush and Jimmy Carter may represent a dying breed. Judging by public tolerance for leaders and heroes who indulge themselves and the popularity of practices like gambling and buying on credit that destroy capital, the end of worldly asceticism may be drawing near.

Other systems of ethics have always supported work, however, and they rise as the Protestant ethic recedes. For the last thirty years, Jews have earned the highest average incomes and attained the highest average levels of education in the United States; they have done this without any history of anxiety over salvation. Irish Catholic Americans, surely unmoved by Protestant approaches to vocation and election, stand second only to Jews in income and education among ethnic and religious groups; the Italians, Poles, and Latinos bring Catholic averages down, but only to a point equal with Protestants.[3] Chinese, Indian, Korean, and Japanese immigrants have worked and succeeded in the United States, without apparently being driven by guilt for original sin or worried about their destinies after death, to a point at which colleges have set up quotas against them.

At the center of the rich complex of values that impels members of these groups to work is the phenomenon called pariah capitalism. Those who know they cannot rely on a culture to support them and who feel themselves to be in hostile or alien territory often respond by working harder. If, like the Jews and like the Chinese in Western nations, members of the group perceive their pariah status as permanent, their work habits will become all the more ingrained.

Jewish pariah capitalism arises from the normal conditions of European history, under which Jews could not own land and so could not depend on the produce of land for security. They had no political rights, so no ruler needed to gain their support; they could not hold university posts, join the officials at court, or apprentice themselves to a guild. If they fell into need, Jews knew they could not rely on charity from the church or from their Gentile neighbors. Their work was their only way to survive. Money was portable; skills were portable; education was portable. Every Jewish father had the Talmudic obligation to make certain that his son knew some trade—anything from tailoring to diamond cutting—that could if necessary be taken with him into exile. Chinese pariah status in the West grows from large differences in language, cultural background, and appearance, and from a racism that often denied Chinese the right to emigrate at all to the nations that periodically expel the Jews. As pariah capitalists, the Chinese have nevertheless flourished all over the world. Chinese, Jews, and other pariah groups also encourage employment and marriage within the group to maximize security and support. But the spectacular benefits that these pariahs confer on each other and on the cultures where they live grow directly from their commitment to work.

Of course, the Chinese in China and the Indians in India do not practice pariah capitalism, but Confucian and Hindu approaches to work, which we will see more in the United States as these groups grow larger and more accepted. The lessening of hostility toward Jews and toward the Irish in the United States has already eroded pariah capitalism among those groups.

For those who belong to no pariah group, the achievements of pariah work ethics might inspire gratitude and imitation, especially with regard to generosity and responsibility within the family and the ethnic or religious group. African American leaders sometimes urge members of their community to practice pariah capitalism. Before turning to the complicated work ethic of those who were brought here as slaves, however, we should appreciate two related approaches to work: that of Catholic peasants and that of evangelical Christians. Most of the hard and anonymous work of the United States—the garbage collecting and the dishwashing, the assembly line and the office cleaning—draws support from cultures alien both to Protestant duty and to pariah adaptation. The peasant work ethic of Southern Europe, Eastern Europe, and Latin America, shaped by Catholic theology and traditional social conditions, has long been ignored by historians of religion, but it constitutes an important aspect of U.S. domestic religion.

"Give me strength," my father would say, often holding his side in response to some pain, as he went to

The person who works

in the spirit of capitalism

never has enough.

At the center of the rich complex of values is the phenomenon called pariah capitalism.

bed at nine or nine-thirty every night of the week. Every morning he rose at four-thirty so that he and his brother could open their grocery store by six. Although my father held a bachelor's degree with a major in biology, the Great Depression led him to return home and to work with several members of his family in the store that his father had started. By the 1960s, only two brothers and one of their wives still worked in the store. Competition from supermarkets made them work harder and harder as they aged, and my father became more and more resigned, fatalistic, and religious.

A more positive exemplar of the peasant ethic, my Uncle Lou loved the grocery business; he loved getting the best fruit he could, displaying it and praising it to customers. Working with him as a child and adolescent taught me how to judge a tomato or an orange, a melon or a grapefruit. Although Lou made fruit baskets into works of art, he was certainly also capable of overselling his stock or of hiding an older item in the middle of the pile. He tended toward frugality, holding down prices and paying me less than minimum wage when I was fifteen years old, before I could work elsewhere. Today, Uncle Lou and my father might be mistaken for entrepreneurs, but they had no dreams for their store beyond making a little money from every transaction. Coming from a farming village on a hillside above Genoa, their approach to work (and to much of life) remained that of peasants who had come to the marketplace.

The power of the peasant work ethic was revealed to me almost twenty years after they sold the store, when my father was eighty-seven years old, and I took him and my mother to one of those farms in Connecticut where people pick their own strawberries. Set before a strawberry bush, Dad turned into a harvesting machine, methodically stripping fruit into the basket, not hurrying but not pausing, apparently tireless, capable of filling two baskets for every one that I filled in my less focused, intellectually abstracted manner. The long absence from the farm made no difference; he immediately sank his ego, his whole consciousness, into the work.

When Dad thought critically about work, he thought not of vocation but of fate; he had five children and the country had a depression, so he remained in the store although he never really liked it. For his children, he hoped not for inspiration or dedication, but for fates that might be better than his own. In the 1950s, when his first son faced a choice between a scholarship to Yale and the Naval Academy, Dad favored the security of the navy; in the '70s, when I said that I was getting a doctorate and becoming a professor, Dad recalled his professors from the '20s and said that I wouldn't make enough money to raise a family (he may be proven right).

Despite my choice of career, the peasant work ethic has continued through my generation. It appears trivially in our gardening and housework, and more seriously in the organizational behavior of people like me, my brothers, and my cousin, Uncle Lou's son, who became a banker. We work with strong loyalty, great reliability, and capacity for institutional heavy lifting—a willingness to take on the harder and less glamorous tasks out of respect for the organization's needs—and, on the negative side (in my own case, at least), with a tendency toward depression and loss of initiative. In place of worldly asceticism, we tend to enjoy excesses of simple pleasures like food and wine and to accumulate things that make us feel more secure.

The rise of immigrants with a peasant (or a pariah) work ethic helps to explain the culture of shopping as entertainment that may soon bury the last worldly ascetic under a mountain of casual clothing, consumer electronics, and prepared food. At the same time, the insecurity and isolation of Weber's Protestant ethic have affected the children of peasants and also those of pariah groups, at least by setting the standards against which we judge our families and ourselves. The dilemma of descendants of peasants in a land of Protestants may cause some of our chronic discomfort with our own economic habits. The nation of Ben Franklin has become addicted to lotteries and to debt.

The history of religion offers alternatives to those caught between the peasant, the pariah, and the Protestant, and tens of millions find such alternative work ethics. Among the most popular is a modern version of what Weber called pietism, a division

The peasant work ethic of Southern Europe, Eastern Europe, and Latin America constitutes an important aspect of U.S. domestic religion.

Pentecostals also dare to hope that God might make them rich.

of Christendom that is now called evangelical, Pentecostal, or charismatic. The pietists of Weber's day and earlier, among them John Wesley and the Methodists, differed from classical Protestants in their confidence that God's grace could cleanse them of all sin, leaving them free from anxiety right now, without waiting for an afterlife. Modern charismatics or Pentecostals agree, but focus their worship on experiencing the Holy Spirit, whose anointing (charisma, including the gifts of healing, prophecy, and speaking in tongues) was first received by the apostles on the holiday called Pentecost, as described in the book of Acts. Much to the scorn of people with money, Pentecostals also dare to hope that God might make them rich. When Pentecostals pray, they seek not simply a relationship with God but results, which makes their prayers look like a superstitious belief in magic to those outside; but these believers say they are in relationship already, so they ask for guidance in their lives and blessings on their work, just as the upper classes can seek help from a mentor or a wealthy parent.

Several Pentecostal religion majors, one student in a master's program, and one who does housepainting and carpentry, have shown me an approach to work disturbingly free of compulsiveness, by ordinary U.S. standards, but capable of engagement in a cause they care about. As Weber noticed about pietists, these Pentecostals are honest and unambitious; Weber saw pietism as the tradition of servants and workers, while the other Protestants, called Calvinist or Reformed, were suited by their traditions to be managers. What has emerged in this country since Weber is the remarkable vocational openness of the Pentecostal. In a marketplace for training and professions as broad as the United States, people who take all decisions to the Holy Spirit may find unexpected success, especially since modern Pentecostals have no aversion to wealth. The mercurial and entrepreneurial preachers who fell in 1988, Jimmy Swaggart and Jim Bakker, are Pentecostals, as is Pat Robertson, who sees himself as called by God to be a TV talk-show host. With the Assemblies of God, the largest Pentecostal denomination, and independent charismatics building new churches in the suburbs, we seem certain to see further elaboration of a Pentecostal work ethic among business leaders.

In government and public service, evangelicals and Pentecostals have been inhibited by their own suspicions of politics and by their working-class origins. As these factors continue to change, their approach to work may displace some of the Protestant individualism and Catholic authoritarianism that has prevailed among workers in politics and government. Jim Wallis, the founder of *Sojourners* magazine, and his staff show that evangelicals and Pentecostals can work for liberal causes, though Ralph Reed and the Christian Coalition worked more effectively, at least in the 1990s. President Clinton has already demonstrated the tireless, enthusiastic communalism—with remarkable freedom from guilt and ascetic tendencies—that people of evangelical background can bring to politics.

Whites, African Americans, and Latinos meet in the churches of the Holy Spirit. In fact, Pentecostalism is the first racially integrated religious movement in U.S. history, and it now leads the expansion of Protestantism in Latin America, Asia, and Africa. Pentecostalism connects the Protestantism of Europe to African Americans, whose powerful but misunderstood work ethic harvested the cotton that made the United States rich in the nineteenth century. Many descendants of slaves work with what might be called a freedom ethic.

In one sense, the enslavement of Africans brought more peasants to the United States, because many of the slaves brought habits from traditional, agricultural societies; but the slave trade also prevented those societies from extending to the United States as European peasant villages did. And some of the slaves were not peasants with traditional religions but Muslims, accustomed to trading with Arabs, or nobles or prisoners of war betrayed and sold to the Europeans by African enemies.

Slavery thrust all of its African victims abruptly into the world of mercantile capitalism, alloyed by little justice or mercy. Yet the descendants of African slaves often approach work more optimistically than the heirs of European peasants, perhaps because African Americans have more faith in freedom. The authoritarian strain bred into Catholic European families by imperial, feudal, and church hierarchies crossed the Atlantic and helped those families to survive in the United States; but the African hierarchies developed less dramatically and disappeared in slavery, leaving Africans to

All of the African, evangelical, peasant, and pariah work ethics have proved invisible.

Often, Jesus undercuts

the value of work.

live out the paternalist fantasies that their masters invented to cover the most nakedly economic exploitation of any population in history. Under this dominion of the Protestant ethic, a spiritual coalescence between African slaves and white pietist workers naturally took place.

In the United States, a new message from some white Protestants, who preached that God's grace was free to all who asked, merged with African musical rhythms and African rituals to encourage possession by spirits. A hundred and fifty years of revivals, beginning in the 1740s, affected both white and black people across a spectrum of denominations and culminated in the birth of a self-consciously Pentecostal movement at the Azusa Street revival in Los Angeles in 1906. The century since Azusa Street has seen the Pentecostal blessings of speaking in tongues, healing prayer, the gift of prophecy, immunity from poisonous serpents, and every other blessing of the Holy Spirit publicly claimed by Christians for the first time since the Christian Scriptures. Working from revival songs to rock and roll, the West African religious heritage has also transformed music and dance in the United States. At the same time, with the great migration of former slaves from South to North, African Americans became synonymous in racist minds with the underclass, the class without a work ethic, the class that needed training to go out to work each day.

Racism keeps a range of social classes together in the African American neighborhoods of northern cities, and racism also necessitates an intense approach to work, a local version of pariah capitalism, among some people in those neighborhoods. Neat storefronts and freshly painted homes stand next to abandoned buildings. Some women do their housework before dawn, leave their babies with their mothers or older siblings, and ride buses across town to care for white people's homes and children; others clean offices at night, while children and husbands sleep, so that they can do child care and housework during the day. More communally oriented than the capitalist norm, African Americans more often share their homes with extended family members, raise the children of friends, or expend much time and energy in building up churches or mosques. As the debate of the late 1990s about ending welfare has shown, slavery also taught

African Americans to keep work in perspective, as a less-than-absolute value, and to resist forced and unpaid labor on principle. African culture, slavery, and racism have combined to make the African American freedom ethic the most complex work ethic now seen in the United States.

All of the African, evangelical, peasant, and pariah work ethics have proved invisible to those who see work through wealthy white eyes and who analyze what they see in terms of Protestant individualism. Understood in such terms, Jewish success results from conspiracy or perhaps genetic heritage; the hard work of Poles, Italians, and Latinos shows their stupid docility; and only white Protestants and those who imitate them really succeed because they know how to work self-consciously and to deny themselves pleasures until they have enough. The idea of working for the sake of the family, so prominent in my father's conversation about himself and in his advice to me, has no place in the systems of John Locke, Adam Smith, or, for that matter, Max Weber. Possibilities such as appreciating work as submission to the rhythm of the harvest or as a way of sharing with others do not even come up.

Yet the inadequacies of dividing work from leisure, individual from family, pleasure from achievement, and vocational choice from destiny—all consequences of the classic Protestant work ethic—appear to anyone with a moment of reflection. Work must have a broader meaning for human life than the concept of vocation can express. As Karl Marx wrote in his youthful, more philosophical days, one can define humanity by religion, consciousness, or whatever one likes; people define themselves by working to create the material conditions for their lives.[4] While other animals live from nature, human beings work on nature and transform it. Marx may not have known how long religions have considered this.

According to two of the oldest religions of the West, humanity was created to work. Stories from the fertile crescent of Mesopotamia, one of the first sites of urban civilization and large-scale agriculture, picture the storm god Marduk forming people out of the mud to work the land as slaves of the gods. An echo of Mesopotamia in the second chapter of Genesis says that before God formed Adam from the ground, no plant had sprung up, because there

Shame impels people to work in Confucian cultures.

Asian work ethics do not center on the individual.

was no one to till the soil. Having made Adam, God set him to work in a garden. Then the meaning of work became part of a curse. Because Adam listened to his wife and ate the fruit of the knowledge of good and evil, according to the third chapter of Genesis, the ground brings forth thorns and thistles, and Adam must eat his bread by the sweat of his face. Although biblical scholars who focus narrowly on texts will not consider it, surely this ancient story carries a memory from the transformation of hunters and gatherers into farmers that happened thousands of years before Genesis was written.

Throughout the rest of the Bible, including the Christian Scriptures, work always remains prominent but has an ambivalent value. For all the texts like those in Proverbs praising diligence, there are others like those in Ecclesiastes saying that work is meaningless. Deep suspicion of cities, merchants, and farmers pervades the Hebrew Scriptures from Genesis through the prophets; good people tend to be shepherds like Abel, David, and Amos, who lead simple lives and presumably work less hard. Often, Jesus undercuts the value of work. When Martha and Mary, the sisters of Lazarus, are hosting the disciples, and Martha complains because Mary is just sitting and listening, Jesus says that Mary has chosen the better part (Luke 10:38–42). In the parable of the laborers in the vineyard, Jesus teaches that God pays everyone the same reward whether they have worked since morning or only for an hour (Matt. 20:1–16). Paul, on the other hand, boasts of making his own living as a tentmaker even though he deserves to be paid to preach (Acts 18:3; 20:33–35).

The Bible does not offer consistent answers or even attitudes regarding work. Small wonder that, with the possible exception of sex (another point of biblical ambiguity), work has become the most problematic of Western values. Equally small wonder that some Westerners have sought healthier attitudes toward work in the religions of Asia. More than guilt, shame impels people to work in Confucian cultures. One difference became evident when George Bush took U.S. auto executives to Japan seeking quotas on Japanese exports of cars in January of 1992; the Japanese wondered in print how chief executive officers like Lee Iacocca of Chrysler and Roger Smith of General Motors could collect tens of millions in a year when they laid off thousands of workers and saw their companies lose money. Being Japanese and Confucian, Toyota or Honda executives would have considered suicide, or at least resignation in disgrace, rather than taking their stock options. Where guilt demands attention to oneself and to abstract norms, like the standards of success or the laws of God or the state, shame arises only in a public context and demands attention to one's relation to a group. To work impelled by shame is to be concerned that others think of one as a good worker. Leaders are not at all exempt from shame; Confucian classical writings consistently admonish leaders to maintain a humane relationship with subordinates.

In the Confucian context there are no absolute heroes in the Western sense, no God or Jesus whose work creates or saves the world. All the world religions that began in Asia see creation as a process arising from impersonal forces. Sometimes, as in Hindu or Shinto traditions, there are many gods; usually there are powerful spirits, as in the ancestor worship of China and Japan or in popular Taoism; sometimes, as in the more severe schools of Buddhism, all thoughts of gods are rejected as distractions from awareness; but the single God of heaven, the God that many Catholics, Jews, and Muslims assume, is not central to Asian religions.

Asian work ethics also do not center on the individual as economic unit. Though success may have as much importance in Asia as in the West, its meaning and relation to work are different. Success in Asia does not come by the grace of some ultimate Capitalist or to individuals who work out their vocations from an individual God. Rather, in Hinduism one works according to one's caste. Even for those like Mahatma Gandhi who have broken from these traditional categories of people, the doctrine of karma teaches that the circumstances of birth and events in life result from a stream of desires, actions, and attachments. To escape unhappiness in this life and a bad rebirth in the next, one of the best courses is to surrender one's ego to one's work. Work with desire or attachment to its results can build egotism, isolating a person and guaranteeing further suffering, both from the loss of loved objects and from the fate of the egotistic soul; but work without attachment slowly chips away the ego and leaves the spirit free. Gandhi always recommended this yoga of work or

Human work may entail more curses than blessings.

We need a new

work ethic now.

karmayoga, especially through simple manual labor like spinning yarn. Inheriting this wisdom from Hindus, Buddhist abbots instruct their monks simply to cook when they cook, letting attention to their work become a spiritual practice.[5]

In the U.S. college where I teach, I advise students to approach their academic work in this way. If they study out of desire for particular results, such as good grades and honors, prestigious jobs and money, or even for the more noble results of self-esteem and individual fulfillment, their work will strengthen their egos and make them more competitive and more liable to suffering; but if they study for the sake of learning itself, attentive not to themselves but to what they are studying, their work can purify their spirits. Real scholars and real artists lose their egos in their work.

Confucian respect for human relations and the Hindu sense of nonattachment, mediated by Buddhist teachers, have met and blended in Korea and Japan. In the competitions for global market share, manufacturing efficiency, and immediate profit, corporations structured by East Asian values have proven themselves at least the equals of the corporate cultures of the West. On the other hand, few people in this country would accept the six-day workweek, the pressure on students and parents, and the lack of room for privacy, creativity, and change that accompany the East Asian work ethic.

We need to start learning from these cultures without either judging them or judging ourselves against them. For example, we could learn to be more aware and more precise. The superior fit and finish of Japanese cars may have something to do with the moment of quiet at the beginning of the Japanese school day. Just sitting quietly for few minutes every day has a great deal to recommend it. If God wanted to speak to us, when would we be able to hear?

A deeper lesson in precision comes from the Taoists, whose monks showed the Buddhists of China (and later of Korea and Japan) how to defend themselves without swords and armies. To develop a sense for the line of least resistance in our work; to become like the butcher in the famous tale of Chuang-tzu, who never had to sharpen his knife because he always put the edge where the muscle divided; this is an ideal that should inform the movements of our bodies, the construction of our buildings, and the planning of our careers. The

Tao Te Ching tells us that the greatest force is like water, which always seeks the lowest place and always adapts to its container, but which wears away the hardest stone.[6] From this perception have come feng-shui, the art of building in harmony with the landscape, as well as judo, karate, and aikido, the martial arts that seemed like magic to Westerners of thirty years ago, but which are taught in YMCAs and schools all over the country today. The West needs such lessons in precision, and we may well be learning them.

Working with the Tao also means working with both the yin and the yang, the female and the male, the yielding and the hard, the dark and the light, the low and the high, the moist and the dry, and recognizing that far from being in conflict, these are all interdependent. One part of the complementary pair cannot even exist without the other. Recognizing the principle of complementarity would resolve the false conflicts between development and preservation, independence and security, even competition and cooperation that prevent us from integrating work into an ideal of economic life. Can development reach its highest potential without preservation, or independence without security? How can the only meaningful competition, the competition to gain the respect of others for our contributions that occurs in all human societies, take place without cooperation?

A more cooperative work ethic could evolve from reverence for the earth. Until people respond with reflexive disgust—the same reflex religions have sometimes succeeded in forming against grievous sins like idolatry and murder, against littering, waste, and pollution—our attitude toward work will be poisoned by the sense that the net effect of human work may entail more curses than blessings on our posterity. Laws and government regulations have already helped to begin this process; but reverence for the earth will not really be part of the domestic religion until corporate executives, board members, and stockholders work with a new spirit, so that we can trust that corporations will no more deliberately or indifferently damage the natural world than they would plan campaigns of armed robbery to raise capital or ignore their legal liabilities in product design.

Fortunately, there are traditions among the religions of the world that can help our domestic religion to

A healthy domestic religion would recognize work as a human right.

Unemployed physicists and chemists represent wasted resources.

forge the commitments that we need. Many people think that the religions of indigenous peoples, especially in North America, have an answer. Some of these nations, especially among the pueblo dwellers of the Southwest, have traditionally thought of themselves as emerging from within the earth, an image that has an advantage of truth over the common Western concept of a God who dropped us here as a test and who will come back for us someday. On the other hand, the much-quoted letter of Chief Seattle about people being part of nature, part of a web we have not woven, may have as little to do with authentic history as Black Elk, whose visionary book speaks in many classrooms for traditional Plains Indians even though Black Elk himself was a Catholic. Historians and anthropologists argue that forests were burned, species driven to extinction, and arid land overfarmed in America long before Europeans came.

Still, the record of the first nations of North America rebukes the white culture of the United States today. Before Columbus, people lived—without the wheel, but with agriculture and astronomy and relative peace—in the Americas for thousands of years (the number is in hot dispute, but no one says less than a few thousand). Rivers in America provided drinkable water when rivers of Europe did not. The forests of England were destroyed before Julius Caesar saw them, but American societies lived in nature without destroying it. When the Puritans came to what became New England, they moved into a world closer to Eden than we can easily imagine. Fish could be taken from the rivers with simple traps; wild turkeys ran in flocks past the front doors of cabins. Now, a few hundred years later, children in Connecticut eat frozen patties made from fish caught off the coast of Peru, processed in South American factories, and shipped thousands of miles with great expense and burning of fossil fuels, because Long Island Sound is too polluted to support a fishing industry, although wealthy hobbyists still catch bluefish and bass.[7]

Such conditions make no sense, even in strictly economic terms, for the vast majority. We need a new work ethic now. Unless we begin to work in reverence for the earth, increasing economic activity may not always increase wealth, let alone happiness or social justice.

From the Jewish and Christian traditions, we could recall that Genesis 2:15, in which God put Adam "in the garden of Eden to till it and keep it," preceded the declarations of Genesis 3:17–19 that the ground would bring forth "thorns and thistles" for Adam, who then had to get his bread by the sweat of his brow. Although work can be a curse, before any curse humanity defines itself by work; and defining oneself as a gardener by nature implies attitudes very different from those of a sweating farmer.

Both political rhetoric about moving people "from welfare to work" and the self-studies of the middle class show increasing tendencies to define people by work. In *The Second Shift* (1989), sociologist Arlie Hochschild pointed out that men would rather work formally, for money, than share child care and housework; she wrote *The Time Bind* in 1997 to argue that women now feel the same way. We want to live at our work as Adam lived in the garden; work has come to be what we are, not simply what we do. Perhaps, as the postindustrial third wave arrives in the richest economies, history is really rolling back toward a garden in which everyone sees work as meaningful. To take the opportunity of this moment will demand collective imagination, a willingness to plan and then to work without becoming mechanical.

Perhaps something analogous to the Confucian motive to work out of concern for avoiding shame and maintaining social harmony will gain new force as technology makes all our lives more public. If people want to work so that they can see themselves and be seen as parts of a community, they may act politically to build communities that provide opportunities for work.

A healthy domestic religion would recognize work—not necessarily pleasant work, but safe, productive, and compensated work—as a human right. The unemployment that we take for granted is actually an incredible, almost unique historical anomaly, a disastrous side effect of capitalism and industrialization. Before stock markets, banks, and capital dominated economic life, there was no such thing as unemployment (with the possible exception of plebeian Rome); in pueblos of the southwestern United States, in African and medieval European villages, everyone had a recognized social function. This began to break down with the land enclosures that drove English peasants to London in the Renaissance, and the breakdown has continued ever since, until today our cities teem with people who either do no work or receive inadequate recog-

Success lies

within the work.

nition for the work they do. As Marx and Engels wrote in 1848, the ruling class of our times has shown itself "unfit to rule because it is incompetent to assure an existence to its slave within his slavery, because it cannot help letting him sink into such a state that it has to feed him, instead of being fed by him."[8]

Meanwhile, those who do have work have less and less leisure, working two and three jobs or longer hours to meet their expenses, or dedicating such time to professional careers that they lose connections with their children and their lives. Everyone lives with radical insecurity with regard to the possibility of environmental disaster, the random nature of violent crime, and the inexorable approach of old age and dependency. Surely unemployed physicists and chemists represent wasted resources in a world fighting for its life against pollution; surely unemployed teachers and holders of doctorates in the humanities and social sciences represent unused strengths as the nation seeks to improve education. With the needs we have for child care, elder care, and health care, any trainable person with a reasonably good will should be able to find work in human services; and the condition of the roads, bridges, and housing stock in older cities means that any able-bodied person should find meaningful physical work. Government could encourage dedication, extending the model of the Peace Corps (or better, the armed services, which pay a living wage) into an Ecology Corps, a Human Service Corps, an Infrastructure Corps. Like the several healing societies that include between them virtually every adult in traditional Hopi or Seneca villages, these agencies could draw support from our whole population. Filling out the empty rhetoric of volunteerism, government could solicit private funding from individuals and from corporations that might wish to target tax payments to particular agencies and projects.

Hopelessness militates against such dreams. If people cannot imagine cleaning up Long Island Sound or taking care of all our children, the thought of engaging in the kind of planning and expenditure necessary to try becomes a nightmare. Here a concept from Hindu tradition may help: to work without attachment to the results of action. Working to care for elders or to rehabilitate housing can never, by definition of the tasks, completely succeed; but in actions like cleaning and caring, success lies within the work.

FOOD   · 4 ·

No matter who does the eating or what they eat, eating mindfully is a religious experience. Food yields an immediate sense of strength; all neurotransmitters hum in response to the power that holds the world together. Such a high has naturally found its place in the formal religions of the world and among the domestic religions of the United States. Depending on the food consumed and the rituals surrounding it, eating can reinforce values ranging from courage to harmony.

Consider the difference between a football team's training table and a Buddhist monastery's rows of rice bowls. Yet in the United States today, one Thanksgiving dinner frequently brings together people with nonrational commitments to the vegetarian restaurant, to the steakhouse, and to the sugar-free, fat-free magic foods of the dieter. Understanding the religion of food demands some sympathy for all these commitments and more.

To eat a steak, for example, is to approach the thrill of cannibalism. Another mammal, related to the mammal whose milk the diner probably drank as a child, has been slaughtered for this muscle. In the mouth, steak chews firmly, yielding a tang of blood and the inherent saltiness of animal life. Slicing off pieces for each bite recalls the skills of the hunter, the butcher, and the sur-

Eating can

reinforce values

geon, professions that ancient authorities including Hippocrates and the Buddha disapproved. If the steak bleeds, eating it violates the Jewish taboo on blood but fulfills the mandate of many primal religions to consume blood for strength. In the postindustrial world, the rarest steak holds the highest status.

According to Claude Lévi-Strauss, author of *The Raw and the Cooked* and other studies, broiled food stands in every culture at the top of a hierarchy, being the cooked food that retains most of the raw power of nature. Roasted food comes next, then baked, fried, and finally boiled. The continuum through the forms of cooking parallels a continuum of resemblances from raw to rotten.[1]

In the domestic religions of the United States, eating steak connects with other hierarchies of value and other rituals, or patterns of behavior. The legends of the West transform the cowboy and the cattle drive into signs of freedom and of white conquest of Native American lands. Through the cowboy, steak gains associations with a football team in Dallas, a style of clothing, a kind of bar, and a way of doing anything from driving an automobile to running a business. Those who drive "like cowboys" or buy and sell stocks "like cowboys" are thought to be likely to eat steaks. They also seem especially "American." In an effort to capitalize on these associations and in response to cultural trends toward disapproval of beef, the beef industry has produced a series of vivid television advertisements, full of Copland music, presenting platters of beef in front of panoramic American vistas. After a few lines about the nutritional virtues and culinary versatility of beef the announcer heartily proclaims, "Beef—it's what's for dinner!"

Alongside beef in the traditional domestic religion of food stand potatoes, turkey, tomatoes, and corn. Native to the Americas, these foods often arrive whole and simple at the table, visibly connecting eating with the harvest. At holiday meals where the civil religion intersects with the domestic—Thanksgiving dinner, or the picnics of Memorial Day, July 4, and Labor Day—such foods predominate. The Thanksgiving turkey has become almost a sacramental food, the totem animal of our national identity. Ben Franklin argued that the turkey, a useful and clean native bird, rather than the eagle, a scavenger associated with the tyrants and kings of Europe, should be our national symbol.

In the practice of a particular region, ethnic group, family, or individual, any food can become sacred. Pizza, the most popular food in the United States, may seem too foreign and too casual to bear religious meaning, but it certainly does so in my own takeout-dependent family. When my son was an infant, my Jewish in-laws often visited us on Friday nights after work, and the pizza I picked up to share with them became the center of a Sabbath meal. The sacred pizza, redolent of family love and leisure, now comes by delivery on Saturday nights, to be consumed (after a blessing) while we watch some variant of the "Star Trek" series.

When people think critically about food, considerations of content can affect the religious experience of eating. Many avoid salt and refined sugar because they seem to influence mood as well as health. Suspicions of inauthenticity—shortening or sugar in bagel flour, artificial coloring in yogurt, monosodium glutamate anywhere—can keep us from committing to a food in our value system, even if we continue eating it for the sake of convenience or because there seems no better alternative in a particular place or time. The traditional domestic religion of food at its best expresses pure thankfulness and exultation, not guilt or desire for self-transformation. Although the cook may feel guilty or responsible if the meal somehow fails, traditional families and other communities sustain their cooks with help and praise, and do not challenge the morality of serving turkey or question the effects of pumpkin pie.

In contrast, for nearly two centuries, an ever-broadening coalition of people in the United States have sought to transform themselves and the world through food. Between Sylvester Graham (1794–1851), who in the 1830s left the Presbyterian ministry to promote whole wheat (Graham) flour, vegetarianism, and total abstinence from alcohol, tobacco, coffee, and most spices, and Dr. John Harvey Kellogg (1852–1943), the founder of the cereal company in Battle Creek and the most famous Seventh-Day Adventist before Michael Jackson, the health food movement grew from a cracker and a series of pamphlets into an industry and a basic change in eating habits in the United States.[2] The creativity of this transformative religion of food becomes apparent in comparison with how the experience

Thanksgiving turkey has become almost a sacramental food.

Blood has sacred power. of eating is managed in other traditions. Building in the space cleared by Christian rejection of food rules, but with a Christian urgency to enter the dominion of God, the modern religion of food in the United States has borrowed from, rediscovered, and added to the values of Jews and Muslims, Indians and Chinese.

Traditional religions often regulate food quite minutely. For observant Jews, the kosher laws make it impossible to eat at all in a nonobservant home or an ordinary restaurant. Many commonly eaten animals are forbidden; to abridge a long list in Leviticus 11, Jews may eat no pork, rabbit, horse, lobster, scallop, oyster, or clam. Blood has sacred power, according to Genesis 9, so both Jews and Gentiles should avoid eating it, and kosher slaughtering and kosher cooking attempt to drain and to cook away any blood from meat. Combining milk and meat, as in a cheeseburger or by eating ice cream after a meal of meat, is so scrupulously avoided that orthodox families have two sets of dishes and cooking utensils, and kosher restaurants specialize either in milk or meat dishes. In the week of Passover, the law forbidding yeast demands that homes be scoured and food discarded or given to Gentiles; often a third and fourth set of dishes and pots, and sometimes a separate kitchenette, is reserved for use at Passover.

The Muslim *halal* rules for food parallel the Jewish *halacha* in forbidding blood, pork, and anything that dies spontaneously, but Islam allows everything from the sea and has developed nothing comparable in complexity to the dietary rules of Judaism. In contrast, Islam is more severe than Judaism in that it forbids alcohol absolutely, and the Qur'an also demands a monthlong fast each year in which Muslims may not eat, drink, or even smoke from sunrise to sunset.

While Muslims use food rules to heighten their consciousness of God, the religions of India impose more general restrictions in service of broader aims. Reflecting India's conviction that the purpose of life is to transcend and escape the process that keeps most souls returning to the world in many incarnations, Hindus of the priestly caste abstain from eating animals. The Buddha arose from the warrior caste and seemed less concerned with purity than with guilt; he taught his followers not to allow any animal to be killed for them, but to accept flesh that was already prepared when offered. The Jains of India, whose teacher lived at about the same time as the Buddha, go beyond Hindus and Buddhists in abstaining not only from animals but from many plants, especially those like potatoes that have to be killed to be eaten or others that are likely to harbor insects that will be killed if the plant is harvested. Seeking absolute harmlessness, holy Jains will sometimes starve themselves to death.

Chinese religion approaches food from another angle entirely. Unconcerned with a supreme God (who has no place in Chinese tradition) or with otherworldly salvation, China focuses on attaining harmony and longevity—at the extreme, even immortality—by eating the right combinations and amounts. Absolutely anything can and will be eaten in China, but the rules for preparing and presenting food reflect millennia of wisdom in which medicine, religion, and the social norms of banqueting form a complex tradition. An effort to balance yin and yang—which is to say the bland and the spicy, the soft and the hard, the wet and the dry, the dark and the light, the female and the male—always informs the selection and proportions on the menu.[3]

All these regulations of food have succeeded in strengthening the overall direction these religions give to life. In the Torah, Jews read again and again that they must keep the law because God wants them to be a holy people. The Hebrew word translated as "holy" is *kadosh,* which literally means "separate," and the kosher laws have certainly contributed to keeping the Jewish people separate from the other nations of the earth. Among Jews who believe in no supernatural force and attend no synagogue, commitments to kosher-style foods and eating habits such as buying bagels on Sunday can become the last link with Jewish identity.

For Muslims, the Qur'an combines concern for health with a command to worship God more fervently by observing laws regarding food; both *halal* rules and the Ramadan fast have surely sharpened Muslim devotion to God. Indian traditions emphasize eating in such a way as to avoid harming other creatures and to relate to this world through compassion rather than attachment; and the Hindu, Buddhist, and Jain traditions have contributed to the world's knowledge of nonviolence as an aim and even as a force. As for China, the great cuisine that emerged from China has flowed through South and East

China focuses

on attaining harmony

and longevity.

In the Christian Scriptures, an ongoing argument about food appears. Asia and established itself even in the West, where the aims of balance, harmony, and longevity were long disconnected from the choice of foods.

The lack of any teaching regarding food in Christianity reflects a break from tradition that has helped to clear the way for the contemporary domestic religion. According to the Bible, Christians only gradually and contentiously gave up the Jewish food laws. Acts 15 records that some of the apostles, including Peter, James, and Paul, met in Jerusalem about fifteen years after the crucifixion of Jesus, and decided among other things to advise Christians to abstain from blood, from animals that had been strangled (rather than slaughtered with a knife, in the kosher fashion), and from any food of which an offering had been made to the pagan gods. Elsewhere in the Christian Scriptures, an ongoing argument about food appears. In Galatians, Paul recounts how he rebuked Peter for inconsistently eating and refusing to eat in non-kosher homes; in Revelation (2:18–20), John of Patmos condemns the church of Thyatira for tolerating those who eat food sacrificed to idols. Ultimately the Christian world decided, with Paul, to "eat whatever is sold in the meat market without raising any question on the ground of conscience" (1 Cor. 10:25).

Yet Christianity took the blessing of the bread (or matzoh) in Judaism, a prayer sanctifying the Sabbath meal and the Passover Seder, into the center of its own worship, and went beyond Judaism in asserting that bread and wine could be material vehicles for divine power (sacraments). In the Prayer of Jesus, Christians ask God to "give us this day our daily bread," referring both to the manna God gave every day to Israel in the wilderness and to the promise that at the end of time, God would feed humanity again in a messianic banquet. Now on the basis of Christian freedom, the domestic religion of food in the United States continues and transforms the tradition of seeking God's dominion at the dinner table.

Animal rights, an important value of this new religion, resonates with the Jewish and Muslim concern for humane butchering and for avoiding certain animals. When respect for the lives of animals leads people to abstain entirely from eating animals, fulfillment of kosher and *halal* rules becomes nearly automatic; the issues of mixing milk and meat and of consuming blood vanish, along with the danger of eating forbidden flesh. Jewish tradition never accepted vegetarianism; to Talmudic moralists, vegetarians seemed excessively righteous, more proud than God wants humans to be. Only recently has a new message broken through. The Holocaust made Isaac Bashevis Singer into a vegetarian by leading him to reflect that with regard to animals, all humans are Nazis.[4] Thinking about the suffering inflicted on animals by modern farming—the calves chained to keep the veal tender, the chickens with beaks and feet cut off, the terrified cattle driven through the pens—has led many Jews and Christians to give up eating land animals and eggs.

Certainly modern, animal-rights vegetarianism connects with Indian attitudes. "Sacred cow" became a term of derision in the centuries when Western thinking could not comprehend why hungry Hindus would not eat their cattle, but now the Indian attitude looks rational (why not have milk and butter for years, from an animal who may also pull your plow, rather than meat for a week?) as well as humane. How many casual eaters of hamburgers in the West would kill a steer themselves; how many could stand in front of a steer or a pig, a turkey or a chicken, and clearly contemplate eating that animal? Although belief in reincarnation still finds few adherents beyond a small group in the United States, something like the Franciscan doctrine that animals have souls has become quite widespread. On the feast of St. Francis, for example, thousands of Christians bring pets and livestock into churches to be blessed.

Yet some doctors raise doubts about the health effects of vegetarianism, and health also forms part of the domestic religion of food. Can vegetarians get enough iron and B vitamins, enough protein of high quality? The traditions of China allow absolutely nothing to escape becoming food under the compulsion of circumstances and in the appropriate amounts to promote health. How many mushrooms and tree molds, roots and sprouts, quail eggs and parts of various animal organs have their place on the Chinese menu or in Chinese medicine! And in this proliferation and this absence of any taboo lies the truth of insubstantiality. The Tao that can be named, seen, or touched is not the eternal Tao. Chinese metaphysics

Animal-rights vegetarianism connects with Indian attitudes.

It can seem that the lion is now lying down with the lamb.

teaches that living things are networks of relationships, energy, and balance, not independent substances whose dignity or purity should keep them from ingesting certain things or from being ingested by others. Without any concern for purity, the classic Confucian/Taoist goals of maintaining harmony and respecting the natural order could at least comprehend abstention from animals raised in the horrors of industrial farming. Chinese values might also add depth to the sensitivity toward the issues of social justice and ecological health raised in the new religion of food in the United States.

For writers like Arthur Simon of the Bread for the World organization and Frances Lappé, who wrote the groundbreaking *Diet for a Small Planet,* the feeding of grain to animals while 20 percent of humanity goes undernourished constitutes a misallocation of resources and a sin that cries to heaven for redress. The concentration of food production by capitalist corporations has disrupted the traditional, subsistence agriculture of much of the world. Peasants who long grew enough to sustain themselves now find the lands they once rented consolidated under foreign or wealthy local ownership and devoted to a single crop, such as coffee, sugar, or bananas, that can be shipped north to the nations of capital. Such foreign trade raises the gross domestic product of the political unit, and so looks good to national governments, the World Bank, and the International Monetary Fund, but there are limits to the amounts of bananas at two and three dollars a pound that customers will buy. When the rich nations stop buying, or find a cheaper source, or the single crop fails, those who once raised their own food face destitution and hunger.

Meanwhile, corporations ship food better produced locally—beer from Japan, for example, or from St. Louis—all over the world, using packaging made of aluminum mined in Peru and burning oil from Arabian wells; they purchase all the materials that they need cheaply, their prices held down by the taxes that support the U.S. military establishment and the Peruvian government. If Sapporo or Anheuser-Busch paid the real cost of making beer in one place and shipping it halfway around the world, without benefit of artificially cheap oil or aluminum, how much would they have to charge for a six-pack? What if the price included the cost of dealing with environmental damage, the pollution and the management of landfills, that results from all that packaging and transportation? Perhaps people would buy fresh local beer in bottles they refilled at the store. Similar dynamics support corporations selling bread, pasta, and breakfast cereals. The apparent freedom of the supermarket conceals other markets, tightly controlled and heavily subsidized markets in raw materials and labor, where the public pays without seeing what it's buying. As the noncommercial before the PBS news hour proclaims, "Archer Daniels Midland, supermarket to the world."

But even if the supermarket aisles of the United States rest on a platform at the peak of a pyramid of injustice, people with authentic religious commitments are still seeking Thanksgiving turkeys, salads for vegetarians, and matzoh for Passover in them, and these foods still serve as materials for authentic rituals, expressing and strengthening real commitments. It might even be argued that the supermarket stands near the peak of the mountain of peace described by the Hebrew prophets. Tomatoes from Israel for $1.99 a pound, still on their vines in the middle of January! Corn and red peppers from Florida, avocados from California, red flame seedless grapes from Chile, daffodils from Ireland at $2.50 a bunch. For people who appreciate their privileges, it can seem that the lion is now lying down with the lamb—or that the potential for millennial abundance makes our failure to set up an efficient way to share even more criminal.

In those same aisles, tens of millions seek magic in the form of foods without the physical consequences associated with fat, salt, or sugar. To a greater extent than is usually acknowledged, this new religion of health and weight control represents a restoration; the corporations encouraged (and still encourage) adding fat, salt, and sugar to breads and soups and cereals to fill out their weight more cheaply and to give them a small addictive twist. The addition of aspartame adds real magic to this religion, however—here is sweetness without calories, a free lunch if it doesn't lead to brain cancer. Those who eat lunch at their desks and get through the workday on one-hundred-calorie yogurt, diet cola, an apple, and a few fat-free pretzels or rice cakes have found a new ideal of purity. For them, the supermarket has become what the city of Vanity Fair was for

Millions seek magic

in foods without

fat, salt, or sugar.

the fleeing Christian in John Bunyan's *Pilgrim's Progress:* a realm of dangerous illusions and temptations in which they must acquire what they need without being sullied.

Easy as it is to mock the food religions of people in the United States, it would be a mistake to overlook developments that may change the world. Two of the first famous American vegetarians, Sylvester Graham and Dr. John Harvey Kellogg, advocated whole grains and invented breakfast cereals because they were concerned for the health of individuals and because they wanted to combat the hereditary degeneracy, transmitted through sex, that they saw as the consequence of an overstimulating diet.[5] Since Dr. Kellogg's death in 1943, the company he founded has largely abandoned its original commitments and has become an engine for delivering sugar and preservatives to children in exchange for profit. Yet people show a continuing, even growing concern for how diet may affect mood; for the ethical dimensions of our food choices; and for the potentials of foods to nurture specific strengths of body and spirit. Hundreds of companies producing health foods continue the industry that Kellogg began in Battle Creek. Diet books consistently top the nonfiction sales charts, and vegetarian restaurants are becoming our era's version of temperance hotels.

In *The Celestine Prophecy*—a fantasy novel that stayed at the top of the *New York Times* bestseller list for two years and in the top ten for four, but which no scholar in religious studies will admit to having read—people become vegetarians so that they can begin to see each other's auras of energy.[6] They send energy to plants to help them grow, not only faster but with more concentrated nutrients, then eat these plants and become even more sensitive. The book also predicts that, by the middle of the next millennium, those humans who have not left this terrestrial sphere will live in many little Edenic gardens in the vicinity of old-growth forests.

Just as *The Celestine Prophecy* had to be privately printed and pushed by its author, James Redfield, and still has not been noticed by the guardians of culture, so the commercial experts are still missing chances for enormous profit in the transformative religion of food. Because people in the United States want to eat their way into the New Jerusalem, an opportunity waits for the right chain of vegetarian fast-food restaurants to become the new McDonald's.

SPORTS · 5 ·

Near the heart of domestic religion in the United States stands the holy trinity of sports: football, baseball, and basketball. Hockey and soccer, golf and tennis, and for that matter mountain climbing, sailing, and skiing all meet religious needs, providing transcendent experience and holding life together for many Americans; but the three team sports that were invented here provide the best ritual expressions of the whole culture's values.

Football players impersonate gods, larger than life and almost invulnerable in helmets and pads, following totems drawn from myth and legend: Giants, Eagles, 49ers, Cowboys. Baseball diamonds organize space on the same principles as the basilica of St. Peter's at Rome, the Temple of Heaven at Beijing, or the Great Mosque at Mecca, and millions of people in the United States spend billions of hours in the contemplative states brought on by staring at those diamonds. In basketball, the same young, emotionally open, and rapidly growing constituency that seeks salvation by losing control in Pentecostal churches takes an ecstatic, semicontrolled high from the fast break and the slam dunk.

All sports promise, and partially deliver, immortality and everlasting youth. As poet Rolfe Humphries wrote, "The crowd and the players / Are the same age always, but the man in the crowd / Is older every season."[1] By

Baseball diamonds organize space on the same principles as the basilica of St. Peter's.

paying adults to develop more complex versions of games that children might play, spectators transform those games into sports and themselves into fans. Fans become facsimiles of children, innocent and expectant, hoping and believing. Or, if a more exalted perspective seems more fitting, they can sit back in timelessness, comparing the young athletes of today against those of distant yesterdays or of tomorrow, as though the fans were gods and only athletes were mortals.

To appreciate how sports connect with and become religious experience, attention must be paid to the details of what happens in the games. The setting and the action of baseball have more numerous and obvious ritual elements than any other sport.

Like Mecca and Jerusalem, Beijing and Rome, every baseball diamond organizes all the space in the world. The foul lines extend forever along the ninety-degree angle they form at home plate, separating a sacred or "fair" quarter of the world, where meaningful action takes place, from the profane or "foul" three-quarters inhabited by fans and nonparticipants. No matter how far Muslims live from Mecca, it matters whether or not they turn in prayer toward the Great Mosque; and so a baseball hit over the fence, out of the stadium, or (theoretically) thousands of miles away would still be fair or foul.

More immediately, the Great Mosque and the baseball diamond also represent the whole world by setting the square of earth within the circle of heaven. The square in baseball is the four bases; in Mecca, the square is the cubical building known as the Kaaba, supposed to have been built by Abraham and visited by the Prophet. At Mecca, the circle of heaven is drawn by a row of columns, and in baseball by the border of grass that arches from first base over second to third. Another square within a circle occurs in St. Peter's basilica at Rome, where a massive square *baldacchino* of brass stands above St. Peter's tomb and the altar where only the pope says Mass, under the circle of Michelangelo's dome. At the Temple of Heaven in Beijing the circle sits within the square so that the earth looks larger than heaven, but this convention of a circle standing for the sky and a square for the earth appears explicitly in the three concentric, circular platforms here, where the boundary of the altar area is a square wall.

At the center of the square formed by the bases of the baseball diamond another circle swells: a low mound of earth reminiscent of the burial mounds of tribal peoples and the stupas of Theravadin Buddhists. In the center of the mound, deeply rooted so that it can be pushed with a man's whole weight without moving, is the rubber slab from which the pitcher throws to begin each act of the ritual. For fans, the rhythmic return of attention to the mound causes the whole diamond to serve as a mandala, a visual pattern that focuses meditation by relating the borders to the center. Nonfans tend to find this rhythm boring.

Action around the diamond suggests an attempt to complete a procession, in which batters, base runners, and fielders perform tasks demanding precise skills and timing according to well-established patterns. As in other sports, fans of baseball quickly learn that the action will fall into categories: the ground ball to shortstop, the long fly caught by an outfielder, the single just over the infield, the double into the gap between outfielders. Routine plays belong to the essence of sports as ritual; but baseball has defined its expectations so closely that some departures from routine can be identified as "errors" and calculated in fielding averages for players and teams.

If the procession succeeds, the batter moves from home to first base, to second, to third, and home again, representing a cycle of life and passing through successive states of mind. At home as a batter, the player is most alert and entirely independent, in single combat with the pitcher and the defensive team. At first base, many decisions lie ahead (whether or not to steal; how far to stand from the base; whether to run on a particular hit; when to stop running), but the player has launched his career and become more dependent on the batter, the manager, and the opposing team. At second base, the runner usually forgets about stealing, takes a longer lead from the base, and relaxes into a kind of midlife; at third, almost no choice remains as the runner stands in foul territory for the sake of safety and waits to be brought home. A successful pilgrim crosses home plate and returns to the dugout, back into the ground to await rebirth. The cycle moves counterclockwise, which is the direction Carl Jung associated with a patient's ego sinking into the unconscious when he saw such a movement

Action around

the diamond suggests

a procession.

A player's time at bat could last forever.

in a dream or a drawing.[2] Catholic priests walking around a coffin before a funeral, people in a church praying at the stations of the cross, and Zen monks processing in the Buddha hall before sitting down in silence all process counterclockwise.

Threes and fours bear the same meanings in the ritual of baseball as in the world's religions. As Jung also noticed, threes everywhere stand for abstract perfection:[3] the Trinity of Christians and of Platonist philosophy; the nine steps between each of three levels in the Chinese altar to heaven; the pyramids, leaning triangles meant to link earth to heaven. Fours mean completeness, or the material world, as in the four directions or the elements of earth, air, fire, and water. And in baseball, every number that concerns abstraction and perfection—the three strikes per batter and the three outs per inning, the nine defensive players, the unbroken string of twenty-seven outs over nine innings in a "perfect" game, in which no one reaches base—is a three or a multiple of three. Only when the fourth is added, when the player walks on four balls or circles four bases to score a run, does anything happen that could end the game and determine a winner.

Adding four and three makes seven, the combination of completeness and perfection, the number of creation. And just as God reached the seventh day and rested, so the baseball fan stands and stretches in the seventh inning.

What Martin Buber wrote about prayer—that prayer does not take place in time, but time takes place in prayer[4]—also holds true for the rituals of baseball. The game has no clock; whether ten minutes or half an hour passes has no more relevance to a baseball game than to a revival meeting, a High Mass, or a wedding. A standard game consists of twenty-seven outs for each team, but any inning can be very short or infinitely long, depending on how much happens, and any game can theoretically go on forever if the batters continue to reach base, if both pitchers keep the other team from scoring, or if the scoring remains perfectly matched on each side. In fact, an individual player's time at bat could last forever, if the player kept hitting foul balls. As the great Yankee catcher Yogi Berra said, "It ain't over till it's over."

Yogi probably never practiced yoga or sat zazen, but his nickname hints at the quality of concentration baseball players share with some who follow Asian religions. In order to hit a small ball speeding at ninety miles an hour from only sixty feet away, a batter needs clear awareness without an object, a state of attention especially cultivated in Zen. If a batter (or, for that matter, a pitcher) has such awareness, and the eye-hand coordination to match, neither excess weight nor lack of height nor slowness of foot matters very much; but (as basketball god Michael Jordan found when he tried baseball) the most accomplished athlete cannot hit without a combination of awareness and coordination that resembles the ideal of Asian martial arts. As Yogi also said, "You can't hit and think at the same time." Sadaharu Oh, the greatest home-run hitter in the history of Japanese baseball, claimed to have practiced his swing with a samurai sword and cleared his mind by sitting zazen.

Now compare the realm of religious experience opened by baseball with that of football. Instead of an infinite mandala the fan sees a rectangle, crosshatched with lines to mark every yard. In place of the halting, often fixed procession of baseball, football offers the conquest of territory by land assault and air strike. With the exception of boxing, no other sport makes knocking opponents to the earth so central to its action; and while boxers can succeed without knocking their opponents down, the defensive team in football cannot. Football is the moral equivalent of war.

Like war, and far more than baseball, football evokes the power of myth. Since ancient times, nations have called on many gods in war and sung their exploits in peace: Marduk of Babylon and Yahweh Sabaoth of Israel, Ares and Zeus and Athena of Greece, Indra of India, to name a few. Football players serve as war gods in our day, standing for the transcendence of self attained through courage, loyalty, cunning, and skill. Where baseball limits competition to one pitcher and one batter at a time, or to a base runner and a few fielders, football demands that whole teams become heroes at once. Those teams tend to bear the names of powerful animals and legendary ancestors—Bears, Rams, Colts, Patriots, Cowboys—rather than adopting the human, faintly self-mocking identities of baseball names such as the Yankees or Dodgers, Red Sox or White Sox, Reds or Mets.

Baseball's power to offer transcendence through beauty springs from an appreciation of timing and

> Far more than baseball, football evokes the power of myth.

Football has most

to do with bonding

to a group.

precision, or from grand vistas such as the peaceful arc of the ball against the sky and the swath of brilliant green grass under the lights; but the beauties of football arise from the pleasures of speed, cunning, and violence. Instead of immediate, naked awareness, football offers the long march of strategy followed by the terror of combat. Coaches sit up nights sketching formations and studying video, then lecture their players on the rationale behind sequences of two dozen plays laid out in advance. Players and fans immerse themselves in charts, formations, and strategies that collapse in a moment as athletes run at each other, leaving bodies scattered on the ground.

Both aesthetically and strategically, football gains much of its power to fascinate from technology: without television, no one could see the details of skill along the line of scrimmage. All the players and the movements of both teams can be captured on a television screen, recorded on videotape, replayed at reverse angle, zoomed into for detail, and frozen for discussion. Before the 1960s and '70s, when television became this sophisticated, football was far less popular than baseball, which can only be seen as a whole at the park. Watching football live has the disadvantage that, even if the fan has the best seat in the house, the line of scrimmage moves with every play, guaranteeing that some important action will happen far downfield.

Yet the bond forged by football has such strength that people will pay to gather outdoors and sit for hours in subzero temperatures or in pouring rain to watch football games that they could see for nothing on TV. Even if baseball fans were willing to endure such discomfort, their sport cannot be played under such severe conditions, so they never bond in the same way. The players on teams also work together more closely in football, as do the owners of professional teams. A combination of collusion between owners, the importance of teamwork in the game, and the shortness of professional careers has kept the movement of individual players by free agency and trades much less important in football than in baseball or basketball. From youth leagues to high school and college, with their pep rallies and homecoming celebrations, football is the major sport that has most to do with bonding to a group.

A critic might well question the values established by these bonds. Being part of a football team means being part of a large, centrally organized hierarchy. Eleven men play offense at once, but only six can legally handle the ball, and eight to ten have the role of blockers for others in any given play. Along the sidelines sit another eleven to play defense, plus scores of substitutes, essential for practices and because of injuries, but marginal in games. Professional teams keep forty-five on their active rosters and more on taxi squads; colleges use junior varsity programs to keep armies on reserve. Coaches of various divisions of the team (quarterbacks, running backs, offensive line, receivers, defensive line, linebackers, defensive backs, special teams for kickoffs and punts) list names above each other on depth charts for each position. Responsibility for the work of every player and coach, beginning in practice and extending to every play called during a game, ultimately rests with a single head coach. Without question, football teaches teamwork, but football teamwork means following directions, not adding and subordinating individual efforts to the whole, as in baseball, or coordinating one's own decisions with others, as in basketball, hockey, or soccer. Football teaches the teamwork of the marching band rather than that of jazz.

The third member of the American sports trinity, basketball, the sport philosopher Michael Novak has compared to jazz,[5] does not touch religion so directly as the patterns and rhythms of baseball or the myths, demigods, and self-immolations of football. Yet religion was present at basketball's birth, in the Young Men's Christian Association (YMCA) of Springfield, Massachusetts.

The triangle of virtues promoted by the "Y"—mind, body, spirit—may well be better served by basketball than by any other major sport. Certainly it provides the best aerobic workout, the exercise that YMCA director James Naismith had in mind when he invented basketball, looking for vigorous indoor activity for young men in winter. More democratic than baseball or football, basketball makes few absolute demands: it requires no esoteric skills such as hitting a small ball with a narrow bat, and no equipment such as pads or helmets. Although five people on a side is the official standard, as few as two can play respectable versions of basketball. Women play basketball far more often than baseball or football. While speed and height are always advantageous, very short (but fast) and very slow (but tall) people sometimes

Religion was present

at basketball's birth

in the YMCA.

The ethics of basketball reflect the perfectionist side of U.S. culture.

compete at the highest professional levels.

As a spiritual exercise, basketball has none of the contemplative purity of baseball and little of the mythic solidarity or militaristic fury of football. In contrast, basketball opens the most direct route to self-transcendence through the ecstasy of absolute athletic achievement. Players rising to the basket for a dunk, running the fast break, squaring off to shoot beyond the three-point arc, or wheeling into a hook shot from the post all execute moves as graceful as ballet and as expressive as modern dance, yet basketball frames these moments in sweat and exhaustion at the level of a half-marathon. Individual players, teams, coaches, and even fans become so closely matched in their drive toward consummation that only the last two minutes of championship games may seem to count; but as in a long jazz set or a Pentecostal service, those who really finish the solo or receive the Spirit have prepared through long rhythms of effort.

The ethics of basketball reflect the perfectionist side of U.S. culture, the same side that gave us YMCAs and the "noble experiment" of Prohibition. Players elbow each other out of the way and knock each other to the floor, but rarely injure each other directly. Unlike in baseball, where a little cheating (a pitcher roughing up the surface of a ball, or a batter filling the inside of his bats with cork) is stopped when discovered—but winked at as part of the game—in basketball every foul an official calls brings play to a halt. Nor can penalties be called by an official but then declined by the opposing team, as in football.

Basketball asks more of its referees than the other two sports. Running constantly, they must look for players taking unfair advantages in the midst of constant bodily contact and minor, inadvertent violations of the rules. They must try to channel the action into a rapid but ordered flow that keeps the game from degenerating into chaotic violence or slowing to a static series of set plays and foul shots. Meanwhile, as part of the perfectionism of the sport, each player stands liable to accumulate too many fouls and to be ejected from the game. Play is affected by the number of fouls a player has long before the actual ejection. Coaches frequently protest fouls, sometimes so vehemently that technical fouls—another example of basketball's perfectionism—are called on them.

At the other extreme of ethical oversight, football referees administer their game in a fashion that would ruin basketball; their whistles start and stop every single play. Referees run the almighty clock; they can pick up the ball and move it fifteen yards or more in the event of a penalty. And although fans of the home team will boo an unfavorable call, in comparison with basketball or baseball, football tolerates very little argument with the referees by coaches or players. Perhaps this relatively peaceful acquiescence results from the collective ethos of football, according to which penalties are called for individual actions but assessed against the team; perhaps it also reflects the referees' need for tighter control over behemoths wearing helmets, with their hands taped into clubs, than seems necessary in relation to men in shorts or double-knit tights.

Baseball umpires rival judges in their dignity. Wearing business attire, not stripes, they do not run on most plays, but normally let the action come to them. And like judges, umpires expect argument. The little knot of livid players and coaches around an umpire, mouths working at a great rate, faces reddening with passion, happens normally in a baseball game. Unless certain magic words are said, or physical contact is made, little comes of the argument; and when any punishment is decreed, it affects the team only indirectly, by the absence of the player or manager expelled. No team gets a free hit or a run, or even moves a runner up a base, because someone challenged the umpire.

Clearly, the details of ethical systems differ from sport to sport. But it is equally clear that the three major U.S. sports together form a broadly practiced, if not always acknowledged, system of ritual and myth, of ways to induce heightened emotions, and of teaching ethics. Hockey, soccer, tennis, and golf also perform these religious functions for some people, but not yet for the culture as a whole. For those who are most engaged, commitment to sports, and to particular players and teams, expresses the basic values of their lives. For many others, engagement with sports holds a secure but marginal place in a set of commitments in which music or art, prayer or cooking may occupy the center. No one follows sports into adulthood without feeling some of their religious power.

Like other religions, the religion of sports has as much potential for evil

No one follows sports into adulthood without feeling their religious power.

The religion of sports has potential for evil.

as for good. What should be done about the power of sports to mold personality, or what the YMCA calls body, mind, and spirit? Football can seem harmful in its essence. If football leaves young people with bodies weakened by disastrous knee injuries, concussions, and broken bones; minds prepared for military and corporate totalitarianism; and spirits entranced by violence and mythology, then perhaps high schools and colleges should not sponsor football. Though baseball seems more benign on the surface, games do take three to four hours to play, and with a season stretching from spring training in March through the various playoffs to the end of October, the sport that was called "the national pastime" bears much responsibility for the mighty waste of time that sports encourages in this country. The Puritan forebears of our culture allowed themselves recreation as a means of relaxation that made them more fit for work; their inheritors come near to making work the evil necessary to acquire money to spend on recreation. Basketball strikes the most vulnerable people, the poor and ignorant and naive in the cities and the country, by holding out a dream of wealth and fame. How many children and young people misuse time and effort that could have guaranteed them success in school, and later in business or in professions, chasing the almost impossible dream of professional basketball?

Traditionally, immigrants and outsiders have won respect through sports. The Irish and Jews proved themselves in the boxing ring and the basketball court during the 1920s and '30s; Italians became Americans as they learned baseball. Jackie Robinson helped prepare the nation to accept civil rights for African Americans. If a substantial number of baseball players from Japan succeed in America, some fans will learn to see the differences between Japanese faces and start to think of the Japanese as human beings. The success of women's college basketball, and perhaps next the women's professional league, represents a real advance in the status of women.

But the other side of this democratizing effect appears in the use of sports to sell products, which tends to stifle political speech and to entangle sports figures in networks of greed. Companies selling beer, sneakers, and cereals have awakened as never before to the power of sports, and these corporations do not want to buy controversy. When Muhammad Ali set new standards for African American assertiveness by telling America that he was the greatest boxer of all time and then, years later, that he had no quarrel with the Vietcong, no one paid him to say so; but Michael Jordan never says a word for which he is not paid. Through sports, Ali became a moral and religious leader and the most recognized human on earth; Jordan may be the most famous person today, but economics might prevent his attainment of moral leadership even if he had the occasion and desire to speak out for some cause. Behind Jordan in today's world of sports stand agents and executives, coaches and college presidents, all collecting six- and seven-figure incomes for promoting basketball as part of a package that enables Nike and other companies to sell expensive shoes to kids who don't need them.

When the basketball coach at a college makes a salary several times larger than the college president's, and collects for a shoe en-dorsement contract on top of that, some priorities have clearly been misplaced. The time has come to regulate sports, to regard sports as a field of expression that affects people at least as profoundly as movies and television drama. We cannot trust the fate of sports entirely to the free market any more than we can entirely trust the market with ed-ucation, because those who win in the market do not necessarily care about us or our children.

Some answers are not difficult to see, though politically they would be difficult to enforce. First, advertising on sports broadcasts should be regulated. Since the audience of sports broadcasts is in-tended to include many children and adolescents, those broadcasts should not advertise beer. Ads for cars and trucks should not show ve-hicles doing dangerous maneuvers. Ads for fast-food restaurants and sugary cereals should be balanced by moments when coaches and ath-letes talk about nutrition and exercise. A much larger percentage of the advertising aired during major sports events should be set aside for public education and public service messages—for voting, against drugs, for education. How can anyone expect people to grow up and work hard at a productive career and to participate in politics if the most compelling images they see as chil-dren tell them to play sports, to get high, and to buy things?

With regard to college athletics, the state and federal governments

> We cannot trust the fate of sports entirely to the free market.

Give coaches tenure

after a normal

probationary period.

should take ruthless action, because the educational institutions that these governments support have become part of a system that corrupts education for many athletes and coaches down to the junior high school level. What benefits come to the state of Connecticut if the University of Connecticut wins a national basketball championship? Do those benefits outweigh the harm done to thousands of distracted and neglected children in Bridgeport, New Haven, and Hartford, children who will not even be recruited for a team that sends scouts—and a highly paid head coach—out across the nation to seek new players? What about the children who are recruited, beginning in junior high in places such as New York, and told that basketball should be the most important thing in their lives? The system will not return to health until it stops serving values set by the corporations and the professional leagues.

History shows that college athletics can be more compatible with education. As recently as the 1960s and '70s, students at academically demanding colleges such as Princeton, Yale, and the service academies could consistently compete near the top of the national level in National College Athletic Association (NCAA) championships and bowl games. The recent success of women's college basketball may relate in part to the sense that these athletes are also students who play because they love their sports, not professional apprentices hired for a few years to wear the uniforms of colleges from which they will not graduate.

Reform might begin with ceasing to give scholarships that require the recipients to play sports; instead, consider sports achievement as one factor among others in assessing an applicant's general merit. Let students who pay their way, or who get scholarships based on their high school activities, their academic strengths, and their financial needs, play on the teams that represent their colleges. Give coaches tenure after a normal probationary period, with salaries on the same scale as professors. Let these coaches teach the games they love, with embarrassment for running a weak program the only penalty for failure. If these steps succeeded, the quality of college athletic competition would decline somewhat. But people would still watch, both live and on television; and with less expensive coaching and recruitment, more of the revenues from sports might go where they should, into the general funds of higher education, to buy books and computers and to heat buildings.

Cities and states should make agreements with each other, and even consider using the power of eminent domain, to take control of professional teams in order to change the corrosively commercial influence that emanates from professional sports. Why shouldn't a general manager hired by a city have as much knowledge and creativity with regard to running a team as a billionaire who never played the game? To cite an egregious case for eminent domain: if it is really true, as the New York *Daily News* reports, that George Steinbrenner pays the city of New York $100,000 a year to rent Yankee Stadium,[6] while pocketing tens of millions from television and all the ticket money and concession revenue from nearly three million fans and billing the city for maintaining the ballpark, the accounting has gone grievously out of balance. For the last half-century, rich people have plundered government budgets to subsidize stadiums, and the networks of roads and public utilities to service them, while holding the right to pack up and leave if the television numbers look better elsewhere or if the lease seems too expensive. The threat of departure becomes a weapon to blackmail voters into approving bond issues and paying for them with taxes.

Under the current system of public subsidy and private profit, marketplace values determine everything associated with the stadiums, and in turn with professional sports in general. Ticket prices escalate, pulled upward by tax-deductible corporate sales; luxury boxes displace ordinary seats; food and drinks are sold at extortionate prices, with every dollar going to private hands. Contracts limit or eliminate public broadcasts of events at these publicly funded stadiums, so that only those with money for and access to cable services, and sometimes to premium channels or pay-per-view listings, can watch at home. In order to command the highest fees from advertisers, who want to reach the largest possible audience of adults with money to spend, basketball championships and World Series games are scheduled to end near midnight, long after the children who most want to see the games have gone to bed. A trend toward corporate ownership of teams threatens to make the situation worse.

Sports at their best can—once did, and still do to an extent—teach children the important but neglected truth that achievements resulting

Sports can teach

important truth.

Only the United States
and the ancient Roman
Empire have made
stadiums so central.

from talent, perseverance, luck, and fair-mindedness make people happier, and in the end matter more, than money. In the sports pages of daily newspapers, fans not so long ago read only about the strengths, weaknesses, and personalities of players and teams and the strategies of managers and coaches. Now whole sports columns, pages, and sections fill with accounts of salary negotiations, licensing fees, product endorsements, and stadium financing. This change of content does involve a healthy increase in realism; money always influenced sports, but the mythographers of the media had less freedom and less inclination to follow that story. It would be hard to argue, however, that the increase in financial realism has not made sports seem less noble, less of a game and more of a business. A better financial story, with profits from city-owned ballparks flowing into neighborhood athletic programs and schools, would help to repair the damage.

Sports also can teach loyalty, to players and to cities, and to the abstract idea known as a Favorite Team, which in many cases stands for the fan's commitment to a set of values. The Yankees' pinstriped dominance; the genteel, stylish losing traditions of the Red Sox and Cubs; and the successful but scrappy liberalism of the Dodgers and Mets have continued through generations of players. In football, commitments to speed, youthful skill, and innovation, or to work, veteran versatility, and conservatism have long separated fans of the Dallas Cowboys and the New York Giants; in basketball, from the 1960s through the '80s the Celtics and the Lakers stood for defense versus offense. Fans of college basketball and football have found well-developed systems of values in the philosophies of the coaches who dominate those sports.

Unfortunately, all of these commitments are by no means healthy. When the Celtics appeared to stand for "white" power in the "black" world of basketball, even if management and players had no such intentions, people rooted for the Celtics for that reason and reinforced their racism. Sometimes the commitments of sports become so intense that they distort other values and lead to actions that go beyond control, as when coaches throw chairs at referees or assault players; sometimes the commitment to victory, power, or personal glory simply allows for no transcendent commitment to fair play or to the rituals of the sport. I think here of the unhealthy commitments of brawlers, bullies, or gamblers such as Woody Hayes, Bobby Knight, or Pete Rose.

In all of history, only the United States and the ancient Roman Empire have made stadiums and spectator sporting events so central to their cultures. The Romans expressed, confirmed, and cultivated their addiction to violence in the arenas that every city built for gladiatorial combats.[7] In our stadiums, we express, confirm, and cultivate our addiction to money. Money can dissolve almost anything, including the commitments of fans to sports. Baseball and football strikes leave fans feeling betrayed and undermine the religious function of sports in giving structure to the year. Autographs are sold rather than given to hero-worshipers, suggesting a parallel with the corruption of saint-worship into a traffic in relics and indulgences at the end of the Middle Ages. Privileges and dangers created by money break the bond between athletes and children that entered our iconography with Babe Ruth. When individual players make more money than whole teams in the same sport, justice and competitive balance in the leagues seem threatened. When average or declining athletes who land in the right places sign contracts for tens of millions, public attitudes shift from personal attachment to impersonal judgment. Identifying with teams or players strengthened certain values in fans, but great social distance based on income deflects fans toward fantasies of ownership in a "rotisserie league" and/or into fantasies of profit through sports betting. Late in June of 1997, I saw a T-shirt with a slogan that may have marked the demise of someone's authentic, religious engagement in sports: "It's not whether you win or lose, it's by how much."

Whether or not the government builds the stadium, citizens should enforce the interest they have in their teams. Players and coaches should realize that the privilege of making a living by playing children's games entails a responsibility to maintain the public stance of role models for children (however conservative, liberal, or radical they may think that those models should be). Everyone, whether sports fan or not, has an interest in our sports rituals being more effective means of building body, mind, and spirit. Taking a warning from the ruined Roman arenas, people in the United States should pay more attention to the religious and moral aspects of what goes on in ours.

· 6 ·   ENTERTAINMENT

Drawing plots from myth and structure from ritual, entertainment—the world of television, popular music, movies, trade books, and glossy magazines that constitutes the most successful industry in the United States—drifts into an age that performers and critics call a new millennium, usually without remembering that only Christians count their years that way or that Jews invented the concept of millennia.

Meanwhile, the community of computers offers a new image of the mind of God. We approach a climax in the process that began with the inventions of motion pictures, sound recording, radio, and television. The new media create "cumulative literacy," in Phyllis Tickle's phrase,[1] capable of supporting new myths in the global village predicted by Marshall McLuhan.

Every time the television, radio, CD player, or computer goes on, a choice with spiritual effects is being made. This has always been the case, but recently the choices have become much more explicit. No one knew what Burns and Allen, the Nelson family, the Honeymooners, Rob and Laura Petrie, or Mary Richards believed about God or the afterlife, or whether or where they prayed or worshiped. Religion came out of the closet into controversy once or twice on "All in the Family" in the mid-1970s; but now characters tend to have identifiable religions, and preachers, priests, and rabbis show up around the edges of many sitcoms and dramas. Who would have dreamt, thirty years ago, that Bob Dylan, the icon of nihilist rebellion in the 1960s, would appear as he did in September of 1997 at a rally for two hundred thousand people before Pope John Paul II, who used the lyrics of "Blowin' in the Wind" to discuss the Holy Spirit?

Far more important, the entertainment world has begun to generate its own religions, or at least cults. Only a reading that takes religion into account can explain "The X-Files" and its spinoff show, "Millennium"; the endless remakes of "Star Trek" since 1966, and the revival release of all three *Star Wars* movies in 1997, twenty years after their first appearance; the appeal of books like *The Celestine Prophecy* and *The Bible Code* to the general public, if not to intellectuals; the persistence of religion-obsessed authors like Alice Walker and John Updike at the center of prestigious prose; the witches, vampires, magic cards, and fantasy games that sprout around every corner; the popular music filled with exhortations to adopt new values by groups called Collective Soul or Nirvana or people like Sting and Sheryl Crow; and the treacly pietism of "Touched by an Angel" on Sundays at eight. Where entertainment once displaced religion, religion now possesses entertainment.

Not that all entertainment touches the realm of nonrational commitments that result in religions. At the circus, performers who traditionally live beyond the bonds of church and state provide pure spectacle and sensation. Dance music from waltzes to the discotheque; screwball comedies from the 1930s and film noir mysteries from the 1940s and '50s; television game shows—the list of nonreligious forms of entertainment seems endless. In the most successful movies, the most popular television shows, and the most popular performers, on the other hand, the sheer force of engagement testifies to the presence of a religious attitude. And the entertainment we choose, even when we choose presumably nonreligious entertainment like the circus, both reveals and affects the values that hold our lives together. How does a circus look to an animal-rights activist, to a feminist, or to an advocate for the physically challenged?

Plays have always had religious power, both positive and negative. In ancient Greece, tragedy honored the gods; in Japan, national myths and legends appeared on stage; in medieval England, mystery and morality plays brought the Christian catechism to life. Then the Puritan

The entertainment world has begun to generate its own religions.

revolution closed down the London theaters. The English colonists in America thought of watching a dramatic performance as a species of idolatry, theaters as a breeding ground of prostitution, and plays themselves as lies. Many people in the United States continued to think so centuries later.

When recording of performances began, the taboo against drama broke down. The movie theaters of the 1920s ended the monopoly of churches in providing stories and models of good and evil in small towns throughout the United States. Because of the movies, actors like Rudolph Valentino, an Italian-born dance instructor who would not have been welcome if he came to most of those small towns in person, became heroes. An industry of entertainment quickly turned all the materials offered by folk tradition and the most engaging aspects of official theology into commodities.

Arguing for his concept of the collective unconscious, Carl Jung wrote that if some disaster destroyed all religions and all records of mythology in the world, while humanity survived, the whole realm of myth and symbol would reappear in a generation.[2] But instead of disaster, the political and technical developments of modern times have released a flood of images reminiscent of Jung's collective unconscious, while at the same time making possible a worldwide consensus that resembles the collective consciousness that sociologist Emile Durkheim ascribed to smaller and more coherent groups.[3] The immigration of fifty million people to the United States over three centuries, the largest migration in the history of the world, mixed all the religions, folktales, and myths of Europe, the Middle East, and Africa; then the industrial and electronic revolutions packaged the results for sale at Disney World, in the video store, and on the radio. To update Jung's metaphor of disaster: the tornado of U.S. history has produced a vacuum of traditional or official culture that sucks archetypes out of the world of dreams and into the marketplace. Many people cling all the harder to their traditions as the storm of images from the U.S. entertainment industry sweeps across the world. But Mickey Mouse and Bugs Bunny, Darth Vader and Barbie connect with aspects of the psyche that will not be denied. They stand for Everyman and the Trickster, Satan and the Virgin in a worldwide, commercial folk religion.

Such modern gods and goddesses inhabit many cathedrals. Disneyland and Disney World have institutionalized what, early in the twentieth century, Henry Adams called "the religion of world's fairs."[4] Setting forth a future of peace and prosperity, world's fairs called people to worship their own creations, and the future soon filled with idols of entertainment. Movie studios and minor (non-Disney) theme parks, fast-food restaurants and Thanksgiving Day parades all display and distribute magical images.

In the religion of entertainment, plays and actors appropriate some of the authority of myth because recordings give them immortality. Clark Gable and Judy Garland might get cancer or commit suicide; Fred Astaire and Katharine Hepburn might grow old and die; but on the screen they will always be the same age, making the same gestures, saying the same words. People not only collect relics from and remember trivia about actors, but also find serious perspectives on the meaning of their own lives by replaying these unchanging, recorded performances. Perhaps the scene showing Gene Kelly singing in the rain, or the goodbye of Humphrey Bogart and Ingrid Bergman in *Casablanca,* has given so much encouragement and strength to so many people that they deserve to be thought of as icons or moments of grace.

Religion also appears in the responses of ordinary people to entertainers. In the case of Elvis Presley, some people become missionaries—tens of thousands of people in the United States have made money impersonating Elvis—or they might make pilgrimages to Graceland, claim to see Elvis and so testify to a resurrection, or seek healings through the immortal star. Smaller cults follow John Lennon, James Dean, and Buddy Holly, among others. When a "new" Beatles song appeared in 1996, millions tuned in to a two-hour special and taped the show, seeking their own meaningful place in history.

Consider how all of this recorded entertainment has affected attitudes toward death in the United States. The makers of the Beatles retrospective canceled John Lennon's death, for themselves if not for him, by mixing the surviving members of the band into a song Lennon recorded. In many movies, from classics like *Topper, It's a Wonderful Life,* and *A Man Named Joe* to minor

Darth Vader and Barbie connect with aspects of the psyche.

The U.S. entertainment

industry has never set

forth an atheistic view

of the world.

modern hits like *Ghost* and *Flatliners,* the dead return, or people journey into the land of death and return to repair their lives. Such serious hope, expressed without irony, rarely or never occurs in films from Europe or Asia; it reflects a nation in which more than 70 percent of the people believe in life after death and 94 percent believe in God, as opposed to figures in the twenties for Sweden and Japan. But perhaps the movies also help to sustain this level of religious faith. Beginning with movie studios run by Jewish immigrants who had to avoid giving offense to an intensely Christian nation, the U.S. entertainment industry has never set forth an atheistic view of the world; it has chosen instead to validate every folk belief from witchcraft to reincarnation to possession by representing such things in vivid colors, many times larger than life.

Science fiction and fantasy can offer entire worldviews, and so can develop religions much more comprehensive than those that emerge from personal stories or celebrity worship. Science fiction normally predicts the future, including the values of the future. By predicting the advances of science and technology, science fiction also implies a metaphysics. Fantasy depends on a realm that approaches religion, the realm of magic—a nonrational quest for knowledge and power regarding the material world based on intuition and resemblance. Blending science fiction and fantasy, the four television series bearing the title of "Star Trek" and the three movies, innumerable books, and computer games from the *Star Wars* series contribute to the values and nonrational commitments of millions in the United States and all over the world.

When the first "Star Trek" series appeared in 1966, it presented a tough but positive, essentially Protestant vision of the future. The United Federation of Planets extended the United States into the galaxy. Updating the platoon movies about World War II, the starship crew replaced the preppy lieutenant, the kid from Brooklyn, and the Southern boy of the 1940s with a Southern doctor (McCoy); a Russian (Chekhov) and a Japanese (Sulu) at the navigation controls; an African American woman named Freedom (Nichelle Nichols, playing Uhura) at the telephone (now subspace communication) switchboard; and a Scotsman named Scott and called Scottie manipulating the engines. A courageous decision resulted in the science officer being cast as an alien—Mr. Spock, from the planet Vulcan, appearing very human except for his pointed ears and his renunciation of emotion—played by a man (Leonard Nimoy) who had been raised as an orthodox Jew. In a sense, Spock functioned as the Morgenthau or Kissinger to his captain: the Jewish intellectual in service of the ruling class. And at the center of this crew stood Captain James T. (for Tecumseh) Kirk, supposedly a native of Iowa—a WASP, in other words, without ethnicity, a real American, bearing the same name as the Kirk, the Presbyterian church of Scotland.

Even more Protestant than Captain Kirk is the mission of the starship *Enterprise*—"to seek out new life and new civilizations; to boldly go where no one has gone before"—but not to interact with these new lives. The Prime Directive of the Federation forbids interference with the development of life on other planets. Like the categorical imperative of the basic Protestant ethicist, Immanuel Kant, which says to act only according to principles that one could will to be universal law, the Prime Directive would paralyze action if it were ever actually followed. And like the Protestant missionaries and traders who encircled the globe, recruiting for Methodism and Mobil Oil as they spread their gospel of universal law, the crew of the *Enterprise* careens through the galaxy in its heavily armed starship, recruiting new worlds for the Federation while pursuing its mission of noninterference. An absolute ideal makes it possible to idealize one's own values absolutely.

At least peace and exploration for its own sake remain the most prominent official values of the Federation, and the *Enterprise* has many adventures that involve no phasers or photon torpedoes. Without question, as Wendy Doniger has observed, "Star Trek" projects the shaman's quest for knowledge and healing into space, while *Star Wars* represents the warfare of good and evil.[5]

Some real Trekkers won't even go to *Star Wars* movies; it seems to them that the adolescent male fantasy, action picture aspects of the plot dominate the science fiction. But the religious messages of *Star Wars* are far more explicit than those of "Star Trek." Where the Federation of Planets con-

The United Federation of Planets extended the United States into the galaxy.

Entertainment expresses religious values more directly than art.

tinues the neutrality of the U.S. government toward religion, the space fleets that clash in *Star Wars* stand for the evil and good sides of a cosmic force that is continually invoked. "May the Force be with you," friends in *Star Wars* say as they depart; the closest "Star Trek" comes to this is the Vulcan expression "Live long and prosper," a purely this-worldly sentiment, although delivered with the splay-fingered gesture of blessing that Leonard Nimoy learned from Orthodox rabbis.

To use the Force one has to open the mind and cease to rely on technology; instructors tell apprentices to reach out with their feelings. Telekinesis, seeing the future, sensing the presence and controlling the minds of others, communing with the dead—who are apparently not really dead, in contrast to the determined agnosticism of "Star Trek" on immortality—all these powers come from the Force. According to the many *Star Wars* books, which extend the story before as well as after the three movies, the Force grows out of life and consciousness. Billions of microbes respond to Luke Skywalker's purity of heart and help bring his light saber to his hand. For those who use the evil side of the Force, anger and hatred forge connections (easier to find and more addictive) with other powers, which are apparently no more or less potent than the powers of light.

Although art often implies a metaphysics—as in the correspondence of Gothic churches to medieval theology or the music of Bach to Enlightenment science—entertainment more directly reflects the cultural consensus, forged by whatever historical, corporate, and/or political powers predominate, about what kind of world this is. Between entertainment and art lies a difference in attitude, because art not only reflects but also consciously confronts the consensus of a culture. The border is blurred—should "the artist formerly known as Prince" be called "the entertainer"?—but art tries to do more, and makes more demands on performer and audience, than entertainment. Art adds to, comments on, deepens, and often attacks the cultural consensus. Art comes from inspiration, insight, genius; entertainment can be turned out by committee, by the routine workers of comedy and drama, even by computer. Exploiting unconscious archetypes and driven by commercial considerations, entertainment expresses religious values more directly than art.

The narratives of contemporary entertainment reveal that four views of history and human nature compete for dominance and provide variety in the domestic religion of the United States today. These worldviews might be called the optimistic, the conspiratorial, the prophetic, and the tribal.

Through the broadest channel flow expressions of the conviction that things are essentially good and that the future will be better, not only technologically but also because human relations will become more just; harmony will increase, and differences will become less divisive. Such hopes inform Disneyland and Disney World; much of the more didactic popular music; television series like "Star Trek" and "Touched by an Angel"; and at the movies, *Star Wars* and the many films that feature magic, from *Ghost* and *Flatliners* a few years back to *Forrest Gump* and *Phenomenon*. No matter what conflicts people face, "the universe bends toward justice," as Martin Luther King preached when he wanted to offer assurance.

In (or on) another channel flows the suspicion that evil conspiracies dominate life and that heroes win only temporarily, as in "The X-Files," in rap and alternative rock, and in the tougher movies that descend from *Blade Runner*. Perhaps a traditional Buddhist could remain optimistic in such a world—I recall hearing a bouncy song that began, "Unstable is the sea of samsara," and went on to describe the universality of suffering, sung by a young man in a Sri Lankan romantic comedy. For most people in the United States, in contrast, fictions of an evil world represent a commitment to heroism for its own sake, a sort of heroic nihilism that helps them to strengthen rather than transcend their egos, or to seek transcendence through humility rather than shared victory.

A third tradition, always in the minority and probably shrinking but still central (especially in mystery writing and in police, legal, and medical dramas), is the view of biblical prophets and those descended from them, such as Marxists, that the world was created good but has fallen under occupation by evil, in the way that Europe was occupied by the Nazis in the Second World War. Eventually good will win, but the passage of time does not guarantee victory. Each person must decide whether to side with the powers of this world—those who kill God's prophets and hold the high positions

The titles of soaps

suggest endless cycles.

Soaps also satisfy the conservative conscience.

of church and state—or with the strong and brave minority of righteous and honest people. When Martin Luther King wanted people to act, he called them to this view of history. Those who really struggle for good in the world often reject all or most of contemporary entertainment, preferring to avoid both the anesthetic effects of Disney and the Force and the destructive negativity of (for example) some rap music and films as violent as *Pulp Fiction*. As the biblical prophets criticized the religions of their day—the temple rituals and priests, the compromises of Israel with pagan customs—so today people with a prophetic worldview dislike most of the domestic religion and prefer art to entertainment, possibly excepting an indulgence in murder mysteries or a favorite television show.

Soap operas offer a fourth worldview, more basic than any historical orientation: the worldview of the prehistoric tribe or of mythic, archetypal religion. Because the story of a soap has no direction and no foreseen ending, soaps have no plot in the classic sense and no overall meaning. For the nonrational commitments of those who follow the soaps, as for many religions outside the Jewish-Christian-Muslim heritage, history does not matter; the world has no beginning or end; and humanity has no meaningful destiny, at least as far as we know. The titles of soaps directly express this ahistorical stance: "As the World Turns," "Days of Our Lives," and "All My Children" suggest endless cycles, while "Another World," "General Hospital," and "Beverly Hills 90210" evoke timeless places. Soaps connect with religious values at the level of direct human relations and types rather than through history. Their stories offer new versions of the permanent communities Americans left behind in the villages of Europe, Africa, and Asia.

In the soaps as in life, within each town and family and individual lurk many drives and affiliations, many jealousies and fears. The plots personify these aspects of psychology. Some characters on a soap act as consistent villains, without regard for others, or actively seek to injure others in struggles for sex and money. Characters such as Larry Hagman's "J.R." from "Dallas," the Alexis Carrington portrayed by Joan Collins on "Dynasty," and at least one figure (such as James Stenbeck of "As the World Turns") on every daytime soap fulfill the religious need for a devil or a destructive trickster. Heroes are less essential, but soaps often feature two or three very attractive people with entirely pure motivations to provide visual interest and victims for the villains. Aside from these extreme types, most of the other characters on a soap function in a low but normal moral range with which ordinary people can identify while feeling morally superior. Most of the characters called "The Young and the Restless," "The Bold and the Beautiful," or for that matter the middle-aged and striving population of soap operas intend to act well, but have weaknesses that lead them to succumb to temptations. Meanwhile, their adventures are observed and their falls cushioned by a chorus of elders, sometimes played by actors who have been with the show for decades, who provide more stability than most U.S. communities can boast.

Often the soaps are denounced as immoral or watched with a vague sense of guilt, because their appeal lies partly in vicarious participation in sexual intrigues and in appreciation of the sex appeal of the stars. But soaps also satisfy the conservative conscience. On a soap (unlike in real life), no one ever gets away with anything. Within a few months, every plot unravels, every theft and every adultery becomes known, and the perpetrators suffer. The fantasy of moral clarity takes place within a larger fantasy of woman-centered sociability. On the soaps, doctors and business executives—more of whom are women than in the real world at present—always have plenty of time to talk, even to fall in love over coffee or at lunch. People drop by at each other's homes and offices. Women have high-powered careers without spending years getting graduate degrees or fighting discrimination because they take time out to have children; and everyone's house is always clean and everyone looks wonderful, no doubt because everyone uses the cleaning and grooming products, advertised for twenty minutes of every hour, that gave these dramas the name of soap operas.

Recognizing the illusions of entertainment leads some people to reject it almost completely. Among the tiny minority of people in the United States who have no television in their homes are three of my clearest-thinking, most fair-minded friends. One of them has a personal history that associates television viewing with substance abuse; he will watch television or go to a movie as a social activity, but watching alone seems as

Recognizing the illusions of entertainment leads some people to reject it.

People who listen

to Top 40 radio stations

will never get over their

last lost love.

empty to him as drinking alone. The second is an art historian and artist who prefers attending the opera or ballet, relaxing in a tub, or clearing the mind with meditation to entertainment; and the third is an orthodox Muslim who stays so busy with teaching, social action, prayer, and family life that he has no time for entertainment (most of which would offend his moral code). Another friend who had lived a year or two in England and has since returned there reacted to the shouting salesmen on our television by saying that what we were watching was not entertainment but punishment.

These people seem to have made correct choices for their personalities; I would not dream of suggesting that they buy a television or watch any particular show. In contrast, my colleagues in the study of religion, especially religion in the United States, who write about healing and the cults of saints but have never seen Madonna or "The X-Files" seem willfully ignorant to me; like the intellectuals Jesus criticized, they try to read the signs of the heavens without paying heed to the signs of the times. Remaining sufficiently engaged with entertainment to follow at least the larger currents in the complicated dream-life of mass culture can help an intellectual remain alert to how mythic patterns work themselves out in life.

Teachers and parents should realize that most young people will reflexively go to the latest big movie and turn on the television, the radio, or the CD player; they need to learn to choose material that will have the spiritual effects they want. As I advise my students in courses called "Sexuality and Religion" and "The Psychology of Mystical Experience," people who listen to Phil Collins and Boyz II Men and Jewel on VH1 and the Top 40 radio stations will never get over their last lost love. Given the commercial purpose of most broadcasting, no one should look for broadcasts of serious drama or news analysis; how much beer and how many trucks can you sell to people in the moods set by serious drama and news? Music and drama and news as they appear in mass media support the same ahistorical, tribal view of life found on the soaps. Fires and floods, accidents, crimes and scandals succeed each other in a meaningless welter of events. On the early and late local news broadcasts, the weather reports, analysis, and forecasts provide the model for all journalism; twenty-four-hour television and radio news channels extend the model of weather reporting to national and international life. My Muslim friend tells me that at his mosque they pray to be delivered from information they do not need. We might also pray not to receive information we cannot understand and do something about. If an Orwellian dictator wanted to use the media to keep power today, he might more easily succeed by overwhelming his subjects with information than by direct lies or repression.

Yet there is hope in the proliferation of channels for seeking and receiving entertainment. At almost every moment of the day, cable systems make some worthwhile information and entertainment available to those who know where to find it; this range of choice was almost unimaginable in the 1950s, when Federal Communications Commission chair Newton Minow looked at what the three networks offered and called television programming "a vast wasteland." And even the non-television owners I know have connections to the Internet; they all send and receive e-mail and search for the information and images they want on their computers. In college in 1970, we fantasized about a television hooked into phone lines and a phonebook full of movies that we could order whenever we wanted. Bill Gates was meanwhile watching reruns of "Star Trek" and thinking about how to get a computer onto every desk. His dream has almost come true, and it will soon make the dream of my roommates possible. Already the computer on my son's desk has access to a great deal more than old movies.

People have predicted the demise of the Internet because no one can make money on it. Now some software companies want to move to an "active desktop" with narrowcasting directed to the needs of particular people. The computer would never be off, but constantly register what the owner selected: perhaps stock or commodity prices, news from Israel, the weather forecast, and the arrival of new e-mail. Liberal commentators say that narrowcasting has already been done by television. And although the convenience of constantly seeing whether or not there is new mail, or seeing whatever one wants to seek on the Internet,

> We might also pray not to receive information we cannot understand and do something about.

The Internet God

is never asleep but

never intrusive.

may satisfy the dreams of CEOs who want to sell something, ordinary people need much more from entertainment than convenience. In making our choices of entertainment, we are to a large degree choosing what moods and emotions, thoughts and fantasies, and even what communities we intend to cultivate. If technology enables people to take control of these choices back from the entertainment industry, a new age may indeed be upon us.

Suppose that the developed nations of the north, and then the rest of the world, attain a universal, liberal democracy and a moderate level of prosperity for all. Prophets from Immanuel Kant and Thomas Paine to Alvin Toffler and Newt Gingrich have been pointing to that goal for centuries.[6] Francis Fukuyama, in his groundbreaking article on the end of history and in a book, has expressed fear that the end of competition between political systems will make life a dull affair, without motives for heroism or the inspiration that produces great art.[7] But even Fukuyama allows that people will still work for recognition by others; he hopes that the Greek thymos, a kind of pride before the community that Plato saw as the motive behind all virtues, may still draw people to work. Predictions that the Internet will collapse unless corporations can make money on it may have missed this recognition motive. Perhaps all those World Wide Web sites and hyperlinks, bulletin boards and chat rooms that colleges, churches, hate groups, pornographers, newspapers, fans of celebrities, and ordinary techies have created will come into their own as a culture beyond money.

Once humanity saw God in natural forces such as the sun and the storm. A few hundred years ago, we added the image of God as a designer and manufacturer—the watchmaker God of the late Renaissance, the Enlightenment, and the Industrial Revolution. Now, in what Alvin Toffler (and Newt Gingrich) call "the third wave," the postindustrial economy of information gives us the Internet as a third metaphor for understanding the basic power that underlies the universe. The Internet God is a universal link, never asleep but never intrusive; this God has an awareness that includes all information at once, though not necessarily applying its knowledge to all situations; this God provides a network in which we all may come to live without losing our individuality.

Already Frank Tipler, a mathematical physicist at Tulane University, has written a massive book called *The Physics of Immortality* to set forth his vision of resurrection within an ultimate computer that constitutes the "Omega Point," where "all timelike and lightlike curves converge."[8] Since all physics can be reduced to information processing, Tipler argues, and since the total number of possible quantum states in a human body is a calculable finite number, humanity will be able to live in the machines that history will bring into being by the Omega Point. Life in these glorified (though some might call them virtual) bodies will be infinitely malleable but continuous with the past, real but perfect, individual but present to the collective. People will choose to modify their bodies in any way they like, and they will also be able to "uplink" with the entire memory of the race. In other words, human destiny amounts to life as entertainment, television transcended by virtual reality and transformed into a comprehensive view of everything, or what traditional theology called the beatific vision.

When I describe Tipler's vision in a class, most people wince, discomfited by the thought of existing forever in virtual reality. His dream raises the question of how much, empowered by computers, the world of entertainment will expand to absorb the whole world of politics and culture, material life and human relations that religion seeks to hold together. A thousand years ago, the act of reading belonged for most literate people to the sacred realm, not to the realm of entertainment. Now politics and medicine, business and scholarship all provide material for entertainment, and practitioners in all these fields carry the attitudes of entertainers into their work. In one sense this is nothing new; shamans always made a good show part of their magic, doctors always cultivated a bedside manner, and religious rituals always approximated theater. Still, when Bill Clinton plays a saxophone on MTV as part of a presidential campaign, new ground is breaking in U.S. politics. My thirty years in higher education have witnessed a real change from the lecturing scholar to the multimedia show in the classroom. Today one virtual Roman Catholic diocese, accessible at www.partenia.fr, has been constructed by a French bishop exiled to Algeria. Should the Christian sacraments become available online?

We will live out

any mythology

we like.

A case can be made that religion and entertainment involve qualitatively different types of engagement. While religion derives from the Latin *ligare,* "to bind," entertainment stems from the French *tenir,* "to hold"; both religion and entertainment can expand to include any human activity, but the religious attitude entails active involvement and trust, while entertainment involves only holding or receiving, with a light grasp of possession. The religious person has bound the self as well as the object, while the entertainment audience can let go instantly. Even the most isolated monks and hermits have usually asserted that some responsible attachment to community remains essential to the practice of religion.

As computers mature and integrate the functions of phones, radios, and televisions, the forms of entertainment may become so vital to our lives that the real binding force of religion runs through them, over circuits and modems. Hospitals and nursing homes have already long depended on television to provide a baseline of companionship; as electronic babysitter, television helped to bring my generation through childhood. Now millions of children own electronic virtual pets from Japan, called "Tamagotchi," or "cute little egg," that have three buttons and a face on a screen. The pets require feeding (both with good food and treats), cleaning, playing, and rest. If well cared for, the pets register happiness on their screens; if neglected, they register unhappiness and eventually die.

What if this went a step further, to virtual friends on the Internet? Interactive programs could show children fictional faces, play with or against them in chess and other games, respond to a list of interests by bringing the children to relevant Internet sites, and carry on e-mail correspondence that might grow into conversation. In Japan, there has been a market for actors playing surrogate families to visit lonely old people; perhaps my generation will visit online with virtual families from our nursing-home beds. At least it should beat television. But if our real families call on our computers, using their digital cameras to appear on the screen and the phone lines to talk, will we be able to tell the difference? One of my colleagues suggests that we will, because the virtual families will be so much more interesting. Long before we have virtual bodies in Frank Tipler's ultimate computer, the difference between virtual and real may blur beyond recognition; we will live out any mythology we like in a virtual dominion of God (or Inferno).

DRINK, DRUGS, AND SOBRIETY
· 7 ·

Discussions of alcohol and drug education, marijuana policy, and recovery programs in the United States reach no conclusions because we never face our religious differences regarding substances. Rituals and values always surround these choices. Jews and Catholics use wine in sacred ceremonies; Muslims, many Protestants, and Theravadin Buddhists abstain from alcohol, but for different reasons. Cannabis (marijuana) can be sacred to Hindus and Rastafarians; many northern Native Americans have taken up peyote; but other people in this country feel so strongly on the other side that possession of these drugs can result in jail sentences and loss of property under state and federal laws.

Before arguing over morality, social policy, or even medical science, we need to think about what kinds of consciousness we want to cultivate. The question demands reflection on how using or not using substances that alter consciousness expresses and affects our traditional religions and our domestic religion—in other words, our basic attitudes toward life, which develop in historical contexts.

Jewish law commands the drinking of wine at Passover and at Sabbath meals; the Hebrew blessing over

We need to think about what kinds of consciousness we want to cultivate.

wine that Jesus said at the Last Supper is still said by millions of Jews every day and in thousands of synagogues on Friday nights. On the holiday of Purim, celebrating deliverance from genocide under the Persians, Jews are advised to drink until they cannot tell the difference between "Blessed be Mordecai" and "Cursed be Haman." Though the Hebrew Scriptures also warn that "wine is a mocker, strong drink a brawler, and whoever is led astray by it is not wise" (Prov. 20), the use of alcohol in Judaism reflects and reinforces the Jewish conviction that the world is good. Psalm 104 blesses God for providing "wine to gladden the human heart."

In contrast, Muslim traditions say that the prophet Muhammad chose milk over honey and wine; the choice is said to have suited the moderate temperament of Islamic religion,[1] which has often tolerated hashish and opium, not to mention coffee and tobacco, even while rejecting alcohol. Many Southern Baptists and evangelicals in the United States came under the influence of a new medical orthodoxy during the nineteenth century, and now see alcohol as so evil that they insist, against all evidence, that what the Christian Scriptures call wine was really grape juice. Theravadin Buddhists abstain for the sake of clarity of mind; not to become intoxicated is one of the five precepts attributed to the Buddha and one of the basic distinctions between Buddhism and Judeo-Christian tradition.

After a campaign of more than a hundred years, led by a coalition of Methodists, Baptists, doctors, and feminists, the United States banned the manufacture, sale, and transportation of alcohol "for beverage purposes" from 1920 until 1933. The experiment, called Prohibition or temperance, failed, but today a spirit of hypersobriety—an attitude Alcoholics Anonymous (AA) members might call real sobriety, as opposed to not drinking—spreads from the circles of AA and through the expanding recovery movement. In this latest version of the temperance crusade, toleration has displaced most of the desire to legislate, but a spirit of evangelical energy and alertness remains.

Meanwhile, the practice of using peyote for vision quests has spread so rapidly among Native Americans in the last century and a half that it now occurs among scores of different nations from Central

America to the Great Plains. Ancient Hindu paintings show the god Shiva sitting at ease under a tree while his wife, Parvati, offers him a mixture of yogurt and *cannabis indica,* the Asian variety of marijuana. And in the late 1960s and '70s, young adults in the United States discovered that the undeclared war in Vietnam and the undeclared war between themselves and their elders at home both connected directly to the spiritual differences between people who drank and people who used hallucinogens and smoked cannabis. Quite apart from any magic in specific substances, the history of religions shows that drink, drugs, and sobriety all serve as well-traveled but quite distinct routes on which humans have sought the transcendence of self. Whatever choices we now make about changing consciousness through substances should reflect an informed sense of which nonrational commitments we want to strengthen and which (if any) we want to foreclose.

The best case for alcohol comes from William James, one of the giants of the first generation in psychology, who praised drunkenness (not simply moderate use) as part of his chapter on mysticism in *The Varieties of Religious Experience.* "The sway of alcohol over mankind is unquestionably due to its power to stimulate the mystical faculties," he wrote, and went on to explain that alcohol enables people to see beyond the "cold facts" and "dry criticisms" that divide the world. "Sobriety diminishes, discriminates, and says no; drunkenness expands, unites, and says yes." [2] What James failed to praise, because he focused exclusively on individual experience, was the communion of drink. By repressing higher brain functions and so releasing inhibitions and enabling people to speak, alcohol turns acquaintances into friends and lovers. It makes ordinary emotions profound and forbidden emotions welcome. A danger arises that the new friends and revelations of alcohol will repeat themselves night after night, becoming banal habits consigned to oblivion or yielding to regret the next day. But no assessment of alcohol should overlook that the Jewish Sabbath blessing and the Christian communion use wine to enhance community, and bartenders do resemble priests distributing their sacraments at the communion rail.

To be fair, William James also knew the price of drink. He saw the

> Drink, drugs, and sobriety all serve as well-traveled routes on which humans have sought the transcendence of self.

Marijuana, television, and meditation each provoke the same kind of electrical activity in the brain.

"poor and unlettered" finding only in alcohol what others found in symphony concerts and literature, and he felt "part of the deeper mystery and tragedy of life" in the condition that "whiffs and gleams of something that we immediately recognize as excellent" should be given to so many "only in the fleeting earlier phases of what in its totality is so degrading a poisoning."[3]

James moved quickly from praising and lamenting drunkenness to a description of intoxication with nitrous oxide, the "laughing gas" that some dentists still employ as a safe means of relaxing their patients. From his own experiments with nitrous oxide, James concluded that "our normal waking consciousness, rational consciousness as we call it, is but one special type of consciousness," and that the other types of consciousness "forbid a premature closing of our accounts with reality." Nitrous oxide set him free to see that mystical states of mind "break down the authority of the non-mystical or rationalistic consciousness, based on the understanding and the senses alone."[4] Without the lesson he drew from deliberately altering his consciousness by using a substance, James almost certainly would not have bothered to collect the thousands of pages of evidence or to write the hundreds of pages of analysis that went into *The Varieties of Religious Experience.*

The whole generation born between 1946 and 1963 in the United States—the baby boomers, whose numbers have so strongly influenced U.S. culture—proved remarkably susceptible to what James called "the anaesthetic revelation."[5] Looking more closely at what marijuana does and what people do with marijuana, it appears that my generation's taste for grass may both result from our early exposure to television and relate to the new appreciation of Asian religions we brought to Western culture. Marijuana, television, and meditation each provoke the same kind of electrical activity in the brain. Crude measurements of such activity long ago yielded crude distinctions between the wakeful, sleeping, and dreaming states. A short and frequent pattern called beta waves appears in ordinary consciousness; a deep and less frequent wave called delta is measured in deep sleep; and during the dreaming phase of sleep, the brain produces a wave called alpha, whose frequency and amplitude fall between the other two.[6] Waking alpha waves occur when people meditate, when they watch television, and when they smoke marijuana.

Could it be that exposure to television in childhood gave those born after 1946 a taste for waking alpha activity that most earlier Americans did not share? Did the waking alpha waves provided by the electronic babysitter prepare us to enjoy marijuana and to practice yoga and zazen? Answers to such questions will almost certainly never come; but we do know that some people do not like marijuana even when they try it, and that many people would not think of trying meditation of any kind. Perhaps these are the same sorts of people who do not enjoy "vegging out" in front of the television, although they may watch for some specific purpose.

Many alpha-resistant types did great deeds in the generation that fought World War II and that led the nation from Kennedy through George Bush. But if waking dreams have no appeal, where can one find a vision of the future, a reconciliation of present contradictions, an insight into what has been repressed or denied? Alcohol helps people to lower emotional barriers and to feel more fully, or at least more sentimentally, what they already feel. But as a depressant, alcohol does not lift people into emotional detachment, enabling them to soar above their problems, or open the mind to new thoughts as reliably as marijuana. If alcohol promotes communion, grass promotes the meditative states where people find something to communicate.

With marijuana, the heart rate increases; people who smoke describe a "high," perhaps some giddiness accompanied by confusion, or a kind of stupidity in the face of complex tasks. Getting stoned would not be good preparation for an argument, while getting drunk can lead to fights. Grass also promotes physical relaxation, not because respiration and heart rate are suppressed but because, as in the alpha state of dreams, the mind becomes more attentive to the body, more willing to lie back and to experience sensations. Sexual inhibitions may be even more drastically lowered by marijuana than by alcohol, but sexual aggression becomes less likely.

This plant named Mary Jane is good for heightening women's sexuality, and for promoting the gentler behavior in men that women often want. Again unlike alcohol, extreme indulgence in marijuana will never cause

Marijuana made

an opening to the

nonrational.

Alcohol served as a

communion of manhood,

not softening but

sharpening the edge.

impotence, although a man who enjoyed sex as aggression and conquest might not like the effects of marijuana. Consistent use increases the proportion of female hormone in men.

As the Kennedy New Frontier dissolved into Vietnam and the civil rights movement ended in Black Power and urban rioting, marijuana supplanted alcohol as the drug of choice for white adolescents and young adults. Some young people expressed amazement that anyone would use alcohol. Drinking seemed an ugly and stupid poisoning of the brain, killing cells, releasing aggression, ending in nausea. In contrast, smoking dope at that time was a political statement and a step in the direction of personal transformation. Politically and personally, marijuana stood for nonviolence. Strange as it seems in retrospect, many people did believe that if the leaders of nations smoked grass rather than drinking, we would have no wars; and while experience has shown that no substance can really bring peace, the perspective still contains a grain of truth regarding alcohol and marijuana. Stoned people are far less dangerous, to themselves and to others, than drinkers.

Most important, marijuana made an opening to the nonrational in a culture that had surely, to borrow terms from William James, prematurely closed its accounts with reality. In these postmodern days, it can be difficult to remember or convincingly to evoke the extreme straightness of the early 1960s. The same years before 1965 that saw the Beatles arrive in the United States and Cassius Clay win the heavyweight championship also put Sergeant Barry Sadler at the top of the popular music charts for months with his "Ballad of the Green Berets." President Kennedy's three challenging, innovative groups for young men—the Peace Corps, the National Aeronautics and Space Administration (NASA), and the Green Berets—all shared a very straight edge and missionary zeal. Alcohol served as a communion of manhood, not in wine but in beer and martinis, bourbon and Scotch, not softening but sharpening that edge. If any large percentage of people in the United States were to see past the cold war and learn the wisdom of yielding to life, of celebrating and sharing rather than competing, working, and judging, it was going to take a few years on something like marijuana to teach them.

What counts as personal transformation can be hard to assess. Everyone who lived through those years recalls people who died, cracked up, or burned out because of drug use that included marijuana, but what happened to the survivors, and to the surviving culture? Among my oldest friends is a lawyer who spent ten years between college and law school pursuing a master's degree in religion and what he now calls "the great white light" at a Zen center. He smoked no grass at the zendo, but without the marijuana of his college and graduate school years he probably would not have considered studying religion in that much depth or sitting zazen. Now he works hard at the law, worries about money and family, and relaxes with alcohol and exercise; but he lives with a more open attitude and converses with me about a greater variety of things than he would have without his grass-induced moratorium. Of course, he would also be richer and otherwise more successful if he had spent those ten years as a lawyer.

Similar questions about perspectives and delays arise when I consider my own past. The grass that I smoked in the 1970s may have helped me to get some of the unconventional insights found in my dissertation, which turned into a fairly successful book. As with my friend, though not as dramatically, some years intervened between having the insights and executing them; I had to stop smoking long before completing the book. As William James might observe, my friend and I and our whole culture probably obtained permanent knowledge of an alternative to ordinary, instrumental thinking because of our experience with marijuana. Listening to the popular music that followed the Beatles' *Sergeant Pepper* album and looking at what has happened to clothing styles, standards of formality in dress, and gender roles, it seems plausible to say that a hard-edged modernity broke up into postmodern chaos, with significant softening of many aspects of culture, and that these changes involved a change of intoxicants. At the same time, politics went into a phase of regression. I remember suspecting, as 1972 turned into '73 and the Christmas bombing of Hanoi brought only a few demonstrators into the streets, that President Nixon was allowing grass to be shipped freely into the country to prevent campus unrest. The rest of the 1970s saw confusion and reaction at the top, while many potential young activists turned into viewers of Chevy Chase and John Belushi on "Saturday Night Live."

Personal transformation

can be hard to assess.

Insidious harmlessness

may also be responsible

for the most acute

damage grass does.

One of the best advertisements that the Partnership for a Drug-Free America has ever produced features a man in his twenties, clearly still living in the bedroom of his childhood and entertaining a friend, getting high on grass. The young man talks about how silly it is to worry about any harm marijuana does; "I've been getting high for twelve years," he says, "and nothing's ever happened to me." Suddenly the front door downstairs slams, and a mother's voice calls up the stairs: "Billy, are you still up there? When are you going to go out and get a job?" The narrator breaks in: "Marijuana. It can make sure nothing happens in your life, too."

Such insidious harmlessness may also be responsible for the most acute damage grass does. Driving intoxicated is never a good idea, but stoned drivers lose less coordination than drinkers. They are more likely to enjoy the scenery and less likely to fall asleep. They become less rather than more aggressive; they need to remember to maintain speed rather than to slow down. Unfortunately, all these mild effects mean that railroad conductors or operators of subway trains who would never dream of getting drunk on the job might think it harmless to get a little high. Most of the time their smoking would in fact be harmless and enjoyable; but grass can lead to confusion, to lapses in concentration that would not occur in a sober person, and therefore to horrible and unforgivable accidents.

Without the obvious penalties of nausea and hangovers, but remaining in the fat cells and the brain for weeks and months, cannabis will always be incompatible with more demanding careers and with the highest levels of awareness. But this does not mean that people caught with marijuana should lose their homes and spend decades in jail cells at a cost to taxpayers of $35,000 a year. If we want a rational policy on marijuana, we should first decriminalize it, allowing people to grow their own but not allowing commercial sales, and make shielding our children from both marijuana and alcohol a high priority of public health. If marijuana were decriminalized but regarded as a public health threat to the young, comparable to polio or tuberculosis, everyone under eighteen could be tested without concern for self-incrimination in schools and at workplaces, and young people could be put in treatment if they repeatedly tested positive. The goal would be to keep people from using marijuana or alcohol until they had mastered reading, writing, basic algebra, and geometry. Pilots and others in critical professions could also be tested routinely, and legal intoxication levels could be established for everyone, but most adults could be left to decide how much they wanted to affect their own consciousness with cannabis from plants that they or their friends grew. No one has ever overdosed or directly died from marijuana, which is after all not a concentrated drug but a weed that grows out of the ground. As the Rastafarians of Jamaica like to quote from from the King James Version of the Bible, God makes "the grass to grow for the cattle, and herb for the service of man" (Ps. 104:14), and "Behold, I have given you every herb bearing seed" (Gen. 1:29).

If decriminalization did not bring chaos after a few years, legalizing and taxing commercial sales of marijuana with limits on advertising would be the next logical step. Cultivating marijuana for smoking and the related plant called hemp for clothing might provide an alternative to the tobacco growers, who supply a substance that raises further religious issues.

Tobacco has caused a great deal more grief than marijuana, and that grief could be lessened by an attitude that confronts its sacred power directly. For millennia, Native Americans used tobacco with no damage to their health. When I hired a Mohawk traditionalist to speak to an adult education group at Manhattanville, he asked to be paid not only in money but with a small pouch of tobacco that I would give him at the speech. Tobacco contains a spirit (chemically, we call it nicotine) that improves short-term memory and helps people to think; it is a substance used in ritual, in this case a respectful greeting and thanks for coming. But the Mohawk specified that I buy tobacco without flavorings or additives. This task was easy but by no means automatic in the world of chewing and pipe tobaccos, and it would be nearly impossible in buying cigarettes.

Before contact with Europeans, Native Americans used tobacco without harm because they used it naturally, not even curing the leaves on racks before smoking them. They added no potassium nitrate to make their tobacco burn constantly and no

Tobacco contains a spirit that improves memory and helps people to think.

Other spirits live in a cactus named peyote and in the mescal bean.

flavorings to sweeten its taste; nor did they roll tobacco up in tubes of paper and carry it with them all day so that they could smoke at will. Instead, at night they passed a pipe around the circle and stimulated themselves a bit with nicotine—a substance that in unconcentrated form would pose no threat, though the delivery systems can be so corrupted by commercial greed as to make people into addicts who kill themselves.

Why not eliminate the most harmful form of tobacco, the adulterated and perverted form it takes in the commercial cigarette? Smokers could roll their own, from tobacco that went out when they did not puff on it. Meanwhile, we should supply cheaper alternative delivery systems for the nicotine that people seek in tobacco: drugstores should sell very inexpensive nicotine patches, gum, and smokeless tubes that supply nicotine in aerosol form to someone who sucks on them. Nicotine candies might be sold by prescription to warn against the danger of overdose, but again they could be sold cheaply. The goal of government policy toward tobacco should be to move people away from addiction and compulsion and toward rational use on the model of the peace pipe and (at most) the after-dinner cigar. Perhaps we would then learn respect for what Native Americans call the spirit of tobacco and return the inspiration of tobacco to our conversations.

Other spirits abused by many white people live in a cactus named peyote and in the mescal bean. People of Mexico and the southwestern United States found long ago that peyote took them to a land of visions; peyote has power far deeper and more demanding than the stimulus of tobacco, the high of marijuana, or the sedation of alcohol. Those who sought this cactus sometimes equated the spirit of peyote with the savior of Christianity because peyote is said to give its life to those who consume the plant. A harsher hallucinogen derived from the mescal bean is often synthesized as mescaline; a fairly mild drug called psilocybin is found in some mushrooms; and LSD or acid, an artificial hallucinogen, emerged from a chemist's laboratory. Coming of age in the early 1970s, I tried mescaline, acid, and psilocybin, or substances purporting to be each of them. For a decade or so after the Harvard psychologists fired Timothy Leary for experimenting with acid, chemical hallucinogens were used by many as a test of sanity and a kind of vision quest. Younger people also used these chemicals to party, as some still do, seeking escape rather than any vision.

Of course, the Native Americans who gather in groups to learn what peyote will teach them as they watch the fire together, then return to their communities to share what they have seen, have much richer contexts for this experience than I found around Cambridge, Massachusetts, in 1972. Despite all the grass we had smoked, and despite sincere desire to explore our minds, we lacked shamans, communities, and rituals. Frightened but wanting to proceed, we fell back on old attitudes and approached hallucinogens with the narrow, intense, and even competitive spirit of white Americans. The first time I tripped, for example, as the drug came on, characteristically distorting the shape of a small white room, the man I was with symbolically held our two suite mates, who were off campus that weekend, in the palm of his hand to show how small and unimportant they were, then dropped them on the floor and stomped them. Although horrified, I also felt some pride that he thought I mattered. After we passed what many then called "the acid test," other friends joined us. On most weekends that spring, and sometimes during the week, we attacked our map of reality with whichever hallucinogen the dealers had soaked into little squares of blotter paper, mixed into pills, or ground up and packed into capsules or soft brown balls of something like halvah. Our aim was to push the limits, whether of sanity or sheer endurance. Once at night the sky turned red, and I could not imagine becoming normal and able to concentrate again. One day I tripped alone, timing myself so that the mescaline came on just before the end of a lecture, and endured hours of wild shifts of distance perception, spatial disorientation, and distorted facial features that left me sitting in a brilliantly lit, ultramodern library trying to follow Jean-Paul Sartre's attempt to unify Marxism and existentialism in *Search for a Method,* while at the same time worrying that my impending heart attack would become a traumatic memory for a girl sitting nearby.

As vision quests, these were childish thrashings of ego; yet that semester produced my first real academic ambition. Probably this would have happened without hallucinogens; but

> The continuing demand for these drugs demonstrates both spiritual need and spiritual courage.

Tales of hallucinogenic transformation became part of the domestic religion among relatively straight people.

the challenge of holding together my mind and my courses added frenetic energy to my quest. I conceived a wildly ambitious idea for a senior thesis that turned out to be beyond my skill, but that yielded good results when my work revealed a more practical topic. I began to see myself as a scholar.

Tales of hallucinogenic transformation became part of the domestic religion, not only for the fans of rock artists such as Jimi Hendrix and Bob Dylan and for those committed to a drug culture, such as Timothy Leary and Hunter S. Thompson, but among relatively straight people as well. Kathleen Norris, the writer and part-time minister who explored the spirit of landscape in *Dakota,* has described a single, negative but transformative experience with mescaline in *The Cloister Walk.*[7] Her account would attract no new users. In the first Manhattan apartment she rented after college, on a Friday after finishing the workweek, Norris and a roommate tried the drug. Apparently shaken by the rush of energy that mescaline provides, and certainly unwise in her decision to try hallucinogens for the first time in such a challenging and unfamiliar setting, Norris panicked and found herself unable to go out, to eat, or to sleep (all common effects of mescaline). She needed days to overcome her terror. Leaving the apartment to meet a member of the Rockettes dance team, who treated her kindly, started the process of recovery; but even weeks later, ordinary objects such as her work shoes could make her burst into tears. Her journal recorded that she needed to learn to live again, one step at a time.

Some ten to fifteen years before Kathleen Norris and I tried it, Republican congresswoman, ambassador, and playwright Clare Booth Luce, the wife of conservative publisher Henry Luce, took acid many times under the supervision of Sidney Cohen, M.D., who later led the drug abuse division of the National Institutes of Health. Luce wrote that acid gave her "a death deliverance experience"; on acid, she learned "that man is so very different from all the other species and yet one with all matter." She concluded that "nature can do nothing awkward, or tasteless," and that "only the human spirit is capable of ugliness."[8] Might we not conclude that part of human ugliness appears in the imprisonment of some people for decades for doing what Clare Booth Luce did with the interest, blessing, and protection of powerful doctors? Acid seems well named to me, because hallucinogens feel as though they dissolve mental connections, removing links in the systems that the mind normally, constantly, and instantly imposes on data from the senses. On hallucinogens, my visions were fleeting and sometimes quite vivid, but never elaborate or profound—for example, one person suddenly had the head of a fish, while another had the head of a horse; a range of nonexistent white mountains once appeared in the distance; the space into which I was walking filled up with a pattern that made it seem solid. On reflection, I think that these effects grew out of isolated features and hints of color that disclosed themselves intensely when they were perceived apart from the connections that normally keep each part of the world bound in relations with others. Applied to habitual thought patterns, such dissolutions may help the mind to liberate itself; doctors have used LSD in therapy for alcoholics. Broken mental connections may not always mend, on the other hand; with hallucinogens, there is no such thing as moderate use.

Reverential use of hallucinogens demands a context of personal support and guidance such as exists today only in some Native American societies, such as the Native American church, but which could develop in the culture at large if the law allowed. The general hunger for mystical experience and curiosity about other people's religions, coupled with assurances about the natural origins and/or purity of the substances, would lead some people to try vision quests with hallucinogens. Certainly, no one should be jailed for using these substances, though those who endanger others by driving under their influence and those who sell them to children should be punished. But should churches—perhaps with medical assistance—be allowed to guide people in exploring consciousness with hallucinogens?

Peyote may be a sacrament, the flesh of God, while acid parodies the sacrament and mescaline poisons those who take it. Without more honest discussion of these drugs by those who have used them for spiritual ends, we may never know. Will guiding people on vision quests become an industry of some Native American nations, as gambling has on some tribal lands? Unlikely as that

> Hallucinogens feel as though they dissolve mental connections.

Cocaine gives

temporary clarity and

confidence.

seems, since political power does not belong to the adolescents, college students, and Native American church members who still use hallucinogens today, the continuing demand for these drugs demonstrates both spiritual need and spiritual courage. A wise policy would warn against casual use of hallucinogenic drugs, educate and test to safeguard our young, but not jail the very few adults who choose to try them.

Cocaine and heroin mercifully missed my college years, although a few grams of white powder found their way to me twenty years ago. Because cocaine so closely resembles the chemicals human bodies make in euphoria, it gives a very pure pleasure to the body and a temporary clarity and confidence to the mind. Never did the bass lines of Gene Wright, the bassist in the Dave Brubeck Quartet, or Pablo Casals playing the Bach cello suites, reveal their richness to me until I heard them with patience and attention augmented by cocaine. Cocaine appealed to thinkers such as Sigmund Freud; Arthur Conan Doyle thought it an appropriate weakness for the fictional Sherlock Holmes. On cocaine the world looks shiny and hard-edged; this is the Cadillac of drugs, conducive to sex with a hedonistic drive but not (like marijuana) for good-natured passivity and exploration.

As with tobacco, in the case of the coca plant Europeans found Amerindians using a leaf (this time by chewing) to stimulate their bodies and to change their moods. Then the Europeans abused the plant, seeking a more intense high and a more convenient package, until they damaged themselves and the lands where the plant evolved. How strange it must seem to Colombians or Peruvians when the United States government sends warplanes and helicopters to destroy coca plants and to combat the habit of chewing coca leaf, scattering fire and herbicide to protect white people from their own compulsions. Stranger still, all this effort results from the European transformation of coca plants, the simple friends of human life for millennia, into a powder and from the pursuit of that powder by Europeans and their descendants with such desire that people steal and kill to possess it, while the money from illicit trade turns criminal gangs into empires and governments into criminal gangs.

Heroin shares with crack cocaine the status of the most feared and hated enemy in the U.S. drug wars. Even those like myself who have never sampled heroin should respect its ancient lineage from the poppy, through the opium that proved so popular among Romantic poets and so destructive when England forced China to accept opium in order to redress a disastrous imbalance of trade. Just as the worst ravages of opium and heroin have been imposed politically, so the best uses of opiates could be politically managed. Heroin may always serve as a vehicle for some prophets of freedom, of alienation, and of nihilism, such as William Burroughs, to make shamanic journeys into and around unhealthy passions, alienation, and death. But violence among teenage dealers, AIDS transmission through dirty needles, corruption of police by drug money, and the corroding effects of U.S. addiction on scores of nations and governments around the world could all become much less prevalent if our politics conceded that the use of opiates is a spiritual practice (although a dangerous one, deserving serious regulations and warnings) and dealt with opiate abuse as a problem of public health.

In making laws and judging ethics, people too easily condemn crimes they have never committed and vices for which they have no taste. A democratic government should not make war on drugs or on any other way that people modify their consciousness; only dictatorships go to war to make everyone feel or think in the same way. If all substances were decriminalized, with manufacture and sale under controls similar to those for alcohol (or under more stringent controls, depending on the substance), the enormous subsidy that drug trade now provides to criminals and the stream of criminals housed and fed in prisons both would cease. Governments, individuals, and groups could express their disapproval of certain substances and of all substance abuse in more plausible, less drastic ways. Realistic advertisements and school programs could teach (for example) that some people have heart attacks the first time they use cocaine and that smoking crack leads quickly to addiction. As with marijuana, the public health interest in ensuring that children maintain the brain capacity to learn basic skills would justify mandatory tests of everyone under the age of eighteen for cocaine and

> People too easily condemn crimes they have never committed and vices for which they have no taste.

The quest for ecstasy through drugs usually leads instead to pain.

opiates, hallucinogens and alcohol, and any other substance widely abused, such as the new phenylethylamine, a chemical relative of both mescaline and amphetamines, called MDMA or Ecstasy.

Ecstasy means far less than other substances in the domestic religion because it has arrived only in the last two decades, and perhaps because adults have been too preoccupied with their own drug histories and recoveries to bother trying it or to notice what the adolescents of the 1980s and '90s have done. Originally used in psychotherapy, Ecstasy has apparently influenced the rise of a whole, heavily technological style of music and dance, exemplified in Madonna's video "Express Yourself," which in turn quotes and updates Fritz Lang's film classic, *Metropolis*. As in *Metropolis* and the Madonna video, which preach that between head and hands the heart must mediate, the most pronounced effect of Ecstasy apparently consists in a heightened empathy and willingness to make eye contact, to touch, and to dance together.[9]

The word *ecstasy*, derived from the Latin for "standing beside oneself," suggests the deepest spiritual need behind drug problems in the United States. In the tradition of Christian mysticism, ecstasy designates the moment when the soul becomes so caught up by internal feelings or visions that the external senses cease to function. At Lourdes in 1854, when Bernadette Soubirous went into the trances in which she claimed to see the Virgin Mary, her lack of reaction to a candle flame near her hand verified that she was in ecstasy. Writers on mysticism place ecstasy in the second of three stages of spiritual life, the illuminative stage, which follows the stage of purgation and flows into the unitive stage.

Behind the compulsive appetites for drugs—the vulnerability to substance abuse that seems so much more acute in the United States than anywhere else—lies an intense and common need for ecstasy among people of the United States. Public displays of ecstasy reverberate through U.S. culture from the invention of religious revivals during the Great Awakening of the 1740s and the outdoor meetings of the 1800s. Losing control, people at revivals notoriously barked and rolled on the ground, spoke in strange tongues, and danced in the Spirit. The 1990s have witnessed a movement among evangelicals that claims uncontrollable laughter as its special mark of the Spirit. The hope for ecstasy descends from revivals to rock concerts by a direct line. In both settings, people seek happiness so intense that it will transcend their bodies. The search for ecstasy drives people in the United States to run marathons, to turn good sexual techniques into moral obligations (as the next chapter describes), and to do drugs.

Unfortunately, the quest for ecstasy through drugs usually leads instead to pain. The round of smoking and drinking, bad trips, and lowered inhibitions belongs to the stage of purgation, where many remain fixed in self-punishment rather than advancing to illumination. Here the domestic religion of the United States provides a dramatic alternative. Alcoholics Anonymous, beginning with two men talking to keep each other from drinking in 1935, now holds meetings every day around the world. Describing itself as spiritual rather than religious in order to be more inclusive, the AA movement certainly fulfills my definition of a religion—a system of nonrational commitments that holds life together—for many who follow its program. At a level deeper than labels, the spiritual practice of AA centers on public confession and surrender in the hope of rebirth, following the model of sin and grace that prevails in evangelical revivals. No one speaks in tongues or falls slain by the Spirit at AA meetings, but intense, authentic emotion is expected.

Mormons, Quakers, traditional Baptists, many Methodists and Lutherans, and the rapidly growing Pentecostal churches are among the U.S. groups that resonate with commitments to sobriety as positive as that found in AA. In the crusade for Prohibition that carried the day between 1920 and 1933, most people in the United States lived in this spirit, or at least believed in supporting it. Since then, the country has added millions of Muslims who do not share the Protestant pattern of rebirth but who cultivate their sobriety with equal intensity.

Evangelists of sobriety and proponents of drugs in the United States both deploy massive economic power and missionary zeal to promote their causes abroad. Most of the world is now buffeted by simultaneous U.S. marketing of tobacco and dire health warnings against tobacco; by our proliferating twelve-step recovery movements and by the prominence of ecstasy in our popular

> The spiritual practice
>
> of AA centers on public
>
> confession and surrender.

culture. The massive U.S. market for drugs and the armies of U.S. salespeople and missionaries have transformed culture and politics from Latin America to the Middle East to Southeast Asia. To the extent that simple joy in alcohol or other substances survives anywhere, it survives as a heritage from other times.

We should certainly hope for better results than holding three hundred thousand people in jail for drug offenses in the United States, mourning millions of dead from substance abuse, and provoking political corruption and drug-related violence around the world. Perhaps mature Americans could admit that we often need or want to change our states of mind; then we could discuss the means and conditions for seeking such change, and begin to turn the points of contention in our domestic religion into strengths. The goal of true clarity of mind, or what AA calls a spiritual awakening—a return from ecstasy or intoxication to the senses, but now with perspectives drawn from the memory of other states of consciousness and with the assurance of a higher power—unites those who use substances and those who abstain from substances in service of awareness, which may be the only indisputable good. (A later chapter on exercise and prayer will explore other ways to clarify the mind.)

Among my college students, there are signs that we many reach a more stable set of values and habits about using substances to alter consciousness. Some of them smoke cigarettes, but none take tobacco for granted or dare to impose smoke on nonsmokers in the ways that my generation did. Today's students also realize that alcohol and caffeine are drugs. Most encouraging to me, not all the straight people among the young are squares. In last year's freshman class, I taught a man who wore black nail polish, sunglasses, and purple hair. When he signed an e-mail message to the class with his name followed by the symbol "sXe", I commented that such a signature probably worked as an eye-catching way to attract sexual partners. He corrected my interpretation, telling me that the symbol stood for "straight edge": no drink, no other drugs, no tobacco or marijuana. Yet as I know from this student's writing and participation in class, his perspective on life needs none of the softening and relativizing influence for which my friends and I turned to drugs in college. Perhaps his children will live in a world that has grown beyond our drug wars and addictions.

SEX, LOVE, AND
FRIENDSHIP

· 8 ·

The search for ecstasy that prepares us for addiction to substances intensifies in sex and affects all of our emotional bonds. Unlike our erratic use and abuse or abstention from substances, our approach to sex, love, and friendship already offers a new vision to the world.

Against all traditions, the domestic religion of the United States upholds freedom, equality, intimacy, and ecstasy as the goals of personal life. These ideals make restrictions on women, gays, and unmarried people look like violations of justice. Adherents of any religious tradition that does not bless anyone's right to make friends with anyone else, to work without limits by sex or gender, to marry any willing partner, or to enjoy a fulfilling sex life face enormous pressure to change in the United States. Through missionaries of our sexual values who work in business, the military, and the media, the same pressure to change reaches around the world.

Nowhere does our domestic religion more clearly distinguish itself, using and discarding the world's religious traditions, than in this personal realm. People in the United States consume the wisdom of India on physical sex, for example, printing pictures of positions

The domestic religion upholds freedom, equality, intimacy, and ecstasy as the goals of personal life.

from the *Kama Sutra* and advice from Tantric Buddhists in supermarket magazines and glossy paperbacks; but we ignore the Indian use of sex to overcome desire and to escape from rebirth, and we reject the Indian context of gender roles and castes. In collision with U.S. values, every tradition contributes and resists. The ancient Jewish concept of building a people leads American Jews to affirm marriage more fervently than most, but more than half of all new Jewish marriages in the United States involve Gentiles. Confucian family ethics survive among some Chinese and Japanese immigrants, but the breakdown of Confucianism now appears in Asian American books and movies about marriage and assimilation. Across every denominational shade of the Christian majority, divorce, feminism, gay rights, premarital sex, and simple hedonism challenge the traditions of monogamy and patriarchy. The struggles of Roman Catholicism with priestly celibacy, the exclusion of women from priesthood, birth control, abortion, divorce, and annulment have made sex and gender the main preoccupation of the Catholic Church in the United States, much to the puzzlement of Catholics in the rest of the world.

Even those least affected by the changes, heterosexual married men, meet new demands and find new rewards with their spouses, with female friends who work with men as equals, and with other men exploring new gender roles. The Million Man March to Washington, D.C., and the football stadiums filled with Promise Keepers show that large numbers of men have been shaken out of complacency. Magazines and advice columns reveal men taking part in the paradoxical but common drive to make personal life simultaneously transformative and reassuring. After the New York Yankees lost their last playoff game in 1997, a column in the New York *Daily News* quoted Yankee manager Joe Torre describing his center fielder, Bernie Williams, as "such a quality individual" that "you want to hug him all the time."[1] Casey Stengel never said that about Mickey Mantle, nor did Joe McCarthy about Joe DiMaggio.

In physical sex, modern people seek ecstasy: we want feeling so intense that it suspends the action of the senses and transcends the boundaries of self. From love, we want nothing less than the fulfillment of life. Surprisingly often, we really do transcend ourselves through sex and fulfill our lives in love. But even when these demands are met, they put great pressure on courtship, marriage, gender roles, and the specifics of sexual behavior. Probably no culture in history has argued more or produced more advice relating to sex and love.

Because we hope for so much, many elaborations of sexual behavior are permitted and many others are prescribed. Mainstream newspaper and television counselors such as "Dear Abby" and "Dr. Ruth" routinely tell women to tolerate their husbands' need to wear women's clothing at home. Evangelical pastors and doctors write books instructing husbands on the most effective way to stimulate the clitorises of their wives before attempting intercourse.[2] Oral sex, once among the specialties for which men went to prostitutes, became a normal means of contraception for the young during the 1970s and a staple of married life as those people became adults and married. The spread of anal sex has been slowed by its association with AIDS, but fantasies of anal eroticism find a much broader audience among readers and viewers of pornography today than they did twenty years ago. Soon—by the time the cultural trend that includes professional athletes appearing on television with transvestites and male action heroes dressing as women in the movies has run its course—anyone who has not gone out in drag and/or tried a same-sex lover may seem old or square.

Behind all the arguments over who does what with whom and when and how, a powerful and revolutionary consensus continues to transform all standards for sexual morality in the United States. In a previous book, I called that consensus "innocent ecstasy." The standard of innocent ecstasy extends across the whole spectrum from evangelicals and conservative Catholics to gay activists and feminists; everyone demands that sex be both as enjoyable as physical capacity permits and also free from guilt.

Ecstatic sex with freedom from guilt became a public moral standard through the work of Margaret Sanger, the founder of Planned Parenthood, and a few psychologists and doctors writing advice books in the 1920s. The cultural leap of the '20s, which brought romance in the movies, love songs on the radio, and opportunities for privacy in and through the automobile to millions,

> We want feeling so intense that it transcends the boundaries of self.

The standard of innocent ecstasy extends from evangelicals and conservative Catholics to gay activists.

as well as more revealing clothing than had ever been permitted in Western history, produced permanent changes in behavior. According to Alfred C. Kinsey, 36 percent of women born between 1900 and 1909 had intercourse before marriage, as opposed to 14 percent of those born between 1890 and 1899. The women who came of age in the '20s also reported more orgasms after marriage, and later generations continued these trends.[3] Now everyone who gives sexual advice, from Pat Robertson to Dr. Ruth to RuPaul, teaches that sex should be as pleasurable as possible for all parties. To enjoy sex is morally obligatory; to present a character in fiction as not enjoying sex is to criticize that character. A confession that sex evokes feelings of guilt or shame will call forth recommendations ranging from reading a book to talking it over in counseling to active sex therapy to spiritual rebirth, but no expert will accept guilt feelings in sex as normal. Whether straight or gay, married or unmarried, or even solitary, sex must be both innocent and ecstatic to be good.

Some roots of innocent ecstasy go back to the 1500s, drawing strength from the original Protestant revolution in domestic values. Rejecting Catholic celibacy, Martin Luther became the first Christian theologian to write about changing diapers and to record his appreciation of the sight of his wife's pigtails lying on the pillow. A century after Luther, the English poet and Puritan John Milton wrote a tract advocating the freedom of Christians to divorce because a loving marriage was so important. During the 1700s and later, John Wesley and the Methodists substituted belief in free grace for the doctrine of predestination that Luther and John Calvin of Geneva had both taught. The new emphasis on freedom led naturally to perfectionism; by the mid-1800s, evangelicals commonly affirmed that God could grant such grace as to deliver people from every impulse to sin, so that they need feel no hatred or lust but only compassion, love, and peace. Going to revival meetings not just to seek salvation but to gain the "second blessing," the grace of perfect love, Methodists and their spiritual offspring in the Holiness and Pentecostal movements directly associated ecstatic experience with freedom from guilt and found their greatest happiness in those moments of revival. Although revivals had nothing explicit to do with sex, both friends and enemies of revivalism have always seen the connection. No one could read the account that Aimee Semple McPherson, a radio evangelist of the 1920s, wrote of her reception of the gift of tongues without seeing a parallel to medical descriptions of sexual arousal and orgasm. When Margaret Sanger attended a Methodist college just before the First World War, she learned straight from her psychology text that the passions could be sanctified.[4]

Popular music made the bridge between evangelical and sexual ecstasy into a highway. From Elvis Presley and Little Richard to Aretha Franklin, Donna Summer, and Michael Jackson, cultural icons for innocent ecstasy emerged from evangelical churches. Jerry Lee Lewis, the early white rocker from Louisiana who sang "Great Balls of Fire" and became infamous by marrying a fourteen-year-old while he toured in England, grew up inseparable from his first cousin Jimmy Swaggart, the singing evangelist who built an international ministry that raised $180 million a year until Swaggart was caught watching prostitutes in a New Orleans motel.

Even those who do not have private detectives ferreting out their sexual kinks sometimes find difficulties in living up to the ideal of innocent ecstasy. Ecstasy demands high levels of performance, and innocence requires that each sex act, or at least each relationship, be capable of being regarded as good. But the worst drawback of innocent ecstasy derives from the antisensual nature of ecstasy itself. According to the definition of an ecstatic state found in traditional books on mysticism,[5] a person in ecstasy is so caught up by visions or sensations manifest to the internal senses that the external senses are blocked. Anyone who has been surprised by marks on the back or the neck after an ecstatic incident knows what this means in sex; for religious mystics, it means that people cannot distract them from their visions, or even that flames held near their hands as they enter trance cause no reaction.

Ecstasy does not include, and may actively reject, sensuality. Today, people often dedicate themselves to pursuing moments of ecstasy (usually identified with orgasm in our sexual value system) while at the same time

> Popular music made the bridge between evangelical and sexual ecstasy into a highway.

Young women became spiritual leaders of the Romantic and modern ages.

despising their bodies. The thin and odorless, youthful and androgynous bodily ideal of our time serves as a natural emblem and vehicle of ecstasy, innocence, and freedom, but hardly of sensuality. Nor has the United States produced any version of a pleasure garden. In place of the geisha houses of Japan, the temples and temple dancers of India, the harems and paradises of Islam, we have pornographic districts and casinos that shut out nature and actively offend the senses, declaring our misgivings about the body. Positive interest in orgasm without sensuality found its ultimate expression in the St. Louis laboratory of William Masters and Virginia Johnson, who used artificial penises, vibrators, and electrodes during the 1950s and '60s to bring women to fifty orgasms an hour. Masters and Johnson led millions to seek multiple orgasms for women, but the quest appeared to entail an attitude more athletic or scientific than sensual.[6]

The modern yearning for freedom and the repression of sensuality both connect to what Jonathan Edwards called "the great Christian doctrine of original sin," the story of Eden and its aftermath that feminists from Elizabeth Cady Stanton to Rosemary Radford Ruether and Elaine Pagels have picked apart and put together over the last two centuries. A drive to overcome original sin, and particularly to prove the innocence of sex, peaked in the decades between the 1920s and the outbreak of AIDS in the '80s. While the Protestant majority in the United States hoped to overcome original sin through the free grace of God, and especially in the ecstasies of revival meetings, Roman Catholic hopes for perfection centered on the Virgin Mary and on modern saints, especially ecstatic women. For millennia, since Paul and Augustine, Western authorities told people to expect to feel shame and guilt in connection with sex; even those who approved of pleasure and prescribed orgasm, such as Albertus Magnus, Thomas Aquinas, and their successors in the Catholic tradition of natural law, held out no hope for innocence on this side of the grave.

Popular sentiment, however, weighed in on the other side. Even in the Catholic world, so dominated by old, celibate men, young women became spiritual leaders of the Romantic and modern ages. Before Bernadette of Lourdes there was Catherine Labouré, the novice of Paris who demanded that a medal declaring Mary to be "conceived without sin" be struck, eighteen years before the church accepted that doctrine. Since Bernadette have come institutions and movements founded by Madeleine Sophie Barat, Thérèse of Lisieux, and Lucy, the visionary of Fatima, among many others. A lesbian separatist, Mary Daly, has now held tenure in theology for twenty years at Boston College; Daly's basic book, *Beyond God the Father,* gives her a strong claim to be considered the most important thinker of the Catholic theological tradition in the United States during the second half of the twentieth century. The ecstasies, the sentiments, and the thoughts of Catholic women have affected their church and the culture in general more than Protestant women have affected their denominations or the world. It seems unlikely that the pop singer and actress Madonna, an Italian American, could have emerged from either a Protestant or a Jewish background, or without the heritage of Catholic devotion to the original Madonna.

In the last two decades, women have led a dramatic expansion of freedom in the moral consensus on masturbation, a behavior condemned by patriarchs from Genesis through Freud. Music videos by women, with titles such as "I Touch Myself" and "Sugar Walls," confirmed the place of masturbation in public discourse. Long before MTV, courageous writers from Shere Hite to Dr. Lonnie Garfield Barbach advocated masturbation as the most reliable way for women to discover their potential for orgasm. Hite knew in 1976 that she was breaking new ground. As she then wrote, "Masturbation is . . . one of the most important subjects discussed in this book and a cause for celebration, because it is such an easy source of orgasms for most women."[7] Hard as it may be for people younger than forty to believe, female orgasm was problematic before masturbation came into the open. Until the 1970s, millions of women in supposedly advanced and liberal cultures lived out their lives without knowing their bodies, wondering why men made such a fuss about sex, sometimes lying back and thinking of duty or something else as they let their husbands do what they wanted, not knowing or caring about their potential to transcend the self through pleasure.

Among men, surveys have always shown more than 90 percent with

Women expanded the moral consensus on masturbation.

Still, male masturbation

is shadowed by a sense

of inferiority and much

justifiable shame.

experience of masturbation; in the 1970s, a survey quoted in a Catholic book on sexual ethics showed that more than 70 percent of college-educated married men continued to masturbate.[8] Responding to this data, the Sacred Congregation for the Doctrine of the Faith reaffirmed the official church teaching that every act of masturbation constitutes a material evil of sufficient gravity to destroy the soul forever unless circumstances such as ignorance, coercion, or mental illness make the person incapable of formal mortal sin. But the tide of innocent ecstasy has engulfed Catholic practice in the United States on this point. Most confessors no longer ask about masturbation, and most Catholics approach the subject as they do birth control, dismissing the church's position as old-fashioned. Still, male masturbation is shadowed by a sense of inferiority and much justifiable shame. Without male masturbation, the industry of pornography, with its almost inevitable exploitation and degradation of women, would disappear. Evangelical Christians condemn the lustful thoughts that accompany masturbation, citing the word of Jesus that anyone who looks at a woman lustfully has already committed adultery in his heart. While many spiritual teachers see an active sex life as compatible with intense dedication, prayer, and perfect love, none that I have found present male masturbation so positively.

A new day may soon arrive, because secular writers are beginning to provide the positive material. In books, magazines, and videos available today, men teach each other to control ejaculation so that they can approximate women's orgasmic capacity. Just as masturbation has begun to seem therapeutic for women, so it may improve men's ability to perform with sex partners. Meanwhile, changes in the nature of sexual fantasy may help men to become less aggressive and demanding within and outside relationships. Pornography without exploitation, deploying literature and art in the mission of breaking down inhibitions, opens possibilities that do not habituate men to the exploitative gaze.

Whether a given expression of sex, on film or in a book, on television or in a live show, is morally good depends on many factors, and the morality of every occasion varies according to how a work is received. During a moment of freedom in the 1970s, I saw strippers at a bar near Syracuse, New York, who had such casual attitudes toward their work and their audience that we learned each other's names. Two nights at that bar, I discovered after returning home, had broken an inhibition I had not known I had against moving my body to music; to my surprise, just watching the strippers taught me to dance. This does not mean I approve of hiring women for stag parties. Even in that bar, one or two of the dancers looked resentful, shy, and exploited. Today, some explicit magazines seem to treat the subjects of their photographs as partners, while others (the vast majority) make no pretense to running anything but photos of objects. Nonexploitative magazines more often run photos of both men and women, and just as often show men alone as women; such equality might become a criterion. But because sex has so much power, even egalitarian erotica will still injure or disturb susceptible people and encourage compulsive behavior in others.

"Don't knock masturbation," said the Woody Allen character in *Hannah and Her Sisters;* "it's sex with somebody I love." Before the scandal of his liaison with Soon-yi Previn, Allen had the status of a moralist regarding sex, and he was one of the few who dealt with masturbation. Among those who have sought to explore desire without abandoning morality, from Sigmund Freud to Allen to Dr. Ruth Westheimer, many have been (at least culturally) Jews. Jews have softened the evangelical edge of innocent ecstasy. In sex as in politics, the tiny minority of Jews in the United States acts as a fulcrum on which the traditional Protestant, Catholic, and evangelical values of the whole culture balance. Jewish tradition disposes people to like sex and to love family life. According to the Talmud, a man of twenty who has not married lives all his days in sin; no celibates, monks, or nuns appear in Jewish tradition, with the exception of the Essene cult that made the Dead Sea Scrolls. The heroes of the Hebrew Scriptures, such as Abraham and Jacob, Jacob's wife, Rachel, and the ancestors of David, Tamar and Ruth, and finally David and Solomon, with their hundreds of wives and concubines, all figure in histories laden with sex.

Most fundamentally, salvation in Judaism comes to individuals through the people; the covenant with God is collective, promising peace and harmony to the world through the his-

Besides being prosexual and profamily, the Jewish influence on U.S. sexual mores has also been protolerance.

> Sex in the movies, as
>
> in Judaism, was untainted
>
> by any inherent evil and
>
> subordinated to love.

tory of a people on a land, and to take full part in that salvation one must have children. When a Christian woman worries over the religion of her grandchildren, she thinks about their everlasting souls; but when a Jewish woman hopes her grandchildren will be Jews, her concern goes beyond the grandchildren themselves to the meaning of her own life, the life of the Jewish people, and the redemption of the world. But besides being prosexual and profamily, the Jewish influence on U.S. sexual mores has also been protolerance. This relates to a general Jewish bias for toleration; especially since the Holocaust, but even before there has been a sense among Jews that when societies become intolerant, they generally make Jews an early target. Despite Judaism's restrictive traditions, for example with regard to homosexuality, surveys consistently reveal Jews as the most tolerant religious group except for Unitarian Universalists (many of whom have an especially liberal Jewish background).

The Jewish influence on U.S. sexual ethics has worked for tolerance through entertainment. From the 1930s through the '60s, Jews owned the movie studios that ran the film industry in this country. In films such as *Holiday Inn,* which featured the Catholic Bing Crosby playing a Protestant and singing "White Christmas," a song written by the Jewish (but married to a Gentile) Irving Berlin,[9] the studio heads subordinated the distinctive features of their own and everyone else's religion to a common U.S. system of values that had a definite role for sex. Sex in the movies, as in Judaism, was untainted by any inherent evil, and no need for the redemption of sex was ever mentioned; it would have seemed pessimistic to associate passions with sin. Having children was as unquestioned a value in the movies as in Judaism. Even when Bing Crosby played a priest, the films did not suggest that his decisions to take and to keep an oath of celibacy implied anything negative about sex, marriage, or family.

While the movies approved of sex, they also firmly subordinated sex to love, and to a model of relationships based on freely chosen monogamy. Lovers selected each other "at first sight" or "fell in love" after verbal sparring, flirting, and teasing; never did they grow into love after their families had arranged their marriages or begin to love each other after having sex under other terms, as sometimes happened in Muslim or Indian harems and in Japanese geisha houses. If a movie depicted an arranged marriage, harem, or geisha house, the story inevitably criticized such customs by bringing them into conflict with the free courtship that people in the United States saw as a natural right, part of their God-given right to pursue happiness.

Those who find each other in freedom and who seek ecstasy without guilt must also be equals. From Elizabeth Cady Stanton, who held the first women's rights convention in a Free Methodist church, to Margaret Sanger to Shere Hite, the frontiers of innocent ecstasy have always been advanced by women. Men have responded, often disapproving of the increased demands that the new model of relationship makes on them. Ultimately, the point of all this struggle over sex has been the transformation of family—the genetic community connected by history, culture, and economics—by friendship. An expansion of absolute intimacy—the gaze of unconditional regard in which people seek God through each other—has proved one of the best results of the redemption of sex through innocent ecstasy.

A renaissance of friendship may surpass and complete the sexual revolution. For the ancient Greeks, friendship was the best model of love; it was through friendship that men discovered their own characters. As Socrates died, he spoke with his friends. According to Plato in the Symposium and the Phaedrus, the love of friends leads to the love of truth and so to eternal life. Now modern America has a chance to make friendship more important, and infinitely more egalitarian in terms of gender, ethnicity, and age, than during that golden Greek age of friendship.

For two centuries, with a few decades of exception, the ruling classes of the West have had fewer and fewer children. Reproductive relationships do not have the importance they did for families and national economies, and the experimentation demanded in modern sex life undermines the permanence of marriage. But friends can remain forever, at the other end of a phone on a lonely night, on a lunch date in the midst of a barren time. Friendships today extend across religious lines, redefining intimacy. Friendship between Christians and orthodox Jews may never include dinner at the

A renaissance of

friendship may complete

the sexual revolution.

Must sex be so

traumatic that friendship

cannot survive it?

Christian home or in their favorite restaurants; friendship with Muslims will involve no New Year's Eve parties or drunken revelations. In other countries and other times, such barriers of custom might have prevented intimacy, but our domestic religion values intimacy too much to relinquish it. We also have more neutral spaces—the commuting automobile, the ubiquitous telephone, the e-mail listserv group, the exercise room—where intimacy can flourish.

The Muslims say that when a man and a woman who could marry, according to age and blood, but are not married to each other spend time together alone, the devil makes a third. Between women and men, traditional wisdom from the Talmud and Catholic moral theology through Billy Crystal's character in *When Harry Met Sally* says that friendship is impossible; sooner or later, the relationship always involves sex. But why have sex with anyone who isn't your friend? And must sex be so traumatic that friendship cannot survive it? The less sensual, more intense ethic of innocent ecstasy has enabled us to find new answers, new problems, and richer situations.

Consider the fantasy world of soap operas. As I wrote in the chapter on entertainment, soaps place their titillating situations within a conservative moral framework where no crime or sexual transgression ever goes unpunished. Corrupt as it may be to enjoy the vicarious thrills of illicit sex without relinquishing self-righteousness, the network of friends and relations that emerges on soaps has a very positive side. All the main characters have married or had affairs with each other; ex-lovers and ex-spouses often carry on friendships and cooperate in child-rearing. Gradual turns in the plot bring sworn enemies together periodically in friendship, business alliances, or sex. Complex patterns of parentage link generations. Maintaining these relationships takes time, and no one on a soap is so busy that time can't be found for a visit over coffee or a long lunch. Careers and business yield to personal life.

Of course, corporations such as Colgate-Palmolive and Lever Brothers sponsor the soaps, and they may indeed act as a fantasy to keep powerless women obsessed with grooming themselves and cleaning their houses; but a second look at soaps discloses the hope for love without limits that lies (perhaps in more ways than one?) at the heart of our culture. Soap operas tolerated gays long before "Ellen" and have for years allowed single people to have sex and love lives; soaps deal with teen sexuality, child abuse, unwanted pregnancy, abortion, AIDS, and even with race and class divisions as they affect love and marriage. Despite being populated with unnatural concentrations of beautiful men and women, these daily dramas mark the expanding tolerance of our ethic of personal life.

Gay thinkers have ascribed many of the changes in intimacy, from the rise of oral sex to the emphasis on friendship, to a homosexual effect on heterosexual behavior.[10] The culture now faces the task of transcending gender, of recognizing that "homosexual" and "heterosexual" are invented categories like "masculine" and "feminine," and that the irreducible differences between genitals need not impact behavior in any preordained way.

Over the last thirty years, biological males and females have come to share many behaviors that once belonged exclusively to one or the other. Long hair for men in the 1960s—"You can't tell the boys from the girls," went the cry—was followed by pants for women not only on weekends, but at school and in the office. "Who wears the pants?" became an obsolete distinction. Women cut their hair short in the 1920s, shorter in the '60s, and in the '90s some got crewcuts. Lately many young, heterosexual men have pierced their ears and a few have put on nail polish.

Still, the culture of the '90s does retain arbitrary gender distinctions in clothing and personal decoration. The skirt, for example—a few feet of material, worn by men in Scotland and as part of a dress in Greece, Pakistan, and many other countries—remains absolutely off limits for men in the United States, at least if they are dressing as themselves and not pretending to be women. Skirts and dresses function as idols or fetishes, examples of magical thinking; these garments define gender as female no matter what the biological sex. Leggings and tunics, a promising unisex garb, have not moved beyond women, even though the look may have been invented by young gay men who wore sweaters and tights in Greenwich Village ten years ago. In my own experiments as a man wearing tights and some variation on athletic gear in many settings, from the supermarket and

Transcending gender, males and females have come to share many behaviors.

Innocent behavior

includes more and more

bodily display.

the bank to the library, the classroom, and even the church, I have found that women generally become friendlier but less sexually attracted to me, while men and preteen girls react along a range from indifference to mild discomfort to pronounced signs of disturbance, such as laughing nervously or looking away. At academic conferences with my middle-aged peers, a long sweatshirt and tights made me nearly invisible. No gay man ever came on to me while I was wearing tights. As for my own emotions, I sometimes felt a bit embarrassed, but more often exhilarated and free, almost reconciled to tasks such as doing the grocery shopping, and often simply comfortable and relaxed. Only when my wife grew tired of seeing me in these outfits did I renounce them.

All the reactions I provoked and felt relate to what parts of the body function as erogenous zones, a concept that connects gender, biology, and sexual style. Leggings produce sensations along the legs and up to the waist, as well as a whole-body consciousness involving posture and movement, that our culture prescribes for women and denies to men. Despite cultural precedents from ancient Greece, the Middle Ages, and the Renaissance, as well as an abundance of nerve endings, the thighs of men have no public role as erogenous zones in the United States.

Meanwhile, the realm of innocent behavior for women includes more and more bodily display. When the concept of innocent ecstasy first came to me in the 1970s, one of the most forceful examples was the babydoll look women adopted in the late '60s, combining very short hemlines with empire waists, light makeup, long straight hair, and unconsciousness of any intent to seduce. The women who dressed that way were usually young and powerless; it should be remembered how few powerful women there were thirty years ago. But in the '90s, female executives, lawyers, and professors can wear skirts reaching only the midthigh in business meetings, courtrooms, or college classrooms. In casual clothing, outfits that once belonged only to showgirls and acrobats now appear in the street. Any man who reacts to what a woman wears by staring, let alone with the more primitive reactions still common in the '70s, will be (rightly) accused of sexual harassment.

Not that we have reached a paradise for women. To be allowed to display one's body can result in regimes of diet, exercise, and even surgery. All women, including those who choose the plainest and most conservative styles, pay dearly for having more freedom than men to dress as they wish, both in the extra money that women must spend on varieties of clothing (all of which carry higher prices than comparable men's garments) and in the time, trouble, and physical discomfort involved in choosing and wearing their clothes. Perhaps such considerations underlie the attachment of some Muslim women to the *chador.* Momentum with regard to gender and sex remains on the side of freedom, however. Before many more years pass, the contest of revolution and reaction that now yields proclamations of sexual preference and celebrities in drag on television, but the same old suits on men in the street, will probably develop into a more practical and tolerant view of what women and men are by nature and what they can do by choice.

As personal freedom claims the whole realm of sex, love, and friendship, the United States may fulfill a process that began more than eight hundred years ago with the troubadour poets who invented Western romantic love in the 1100s. For most of history, most people lived the way people in tribal or traditional societies live today. Born into the commitments of their families, they married and had sex because these were good things to do on both socioeconomic and biological levels. People who married in this way did not think of life in terms of individual fulfillment, although some of them accomplished extraordinary things in religion, art, or politics. Joseph Campbell said that the birth of romantic love in the twelfth century brought individualism into the world; he cited Tristan and Isolde as the first story that presented its heroes as admirable because they preferred each other to the laws of their country and their God, courting damnation for love.[11]

Long before romantic love made marriage a free expression of the spirit, however, individualism flourished in the friendships of those devoted to the truth. From Athens and the arhats of the Buddha, from the schools of the Hebrew prophets and the circle of friends who speak in the works of Confucius, down through the male and female disciples of Jesus and the medieval monks and nuns who sometimes married each other in the

The Buddha, Socrates, and Jesus asked people to love unsentimentally.

same-sex ceremonies discovered by John Boswell,[12] those who sought the infinite often found it by looking through each other's eyes. Not within the eyes but through them: sentimental, possessive attachment to other people may feel wonderful, but it does not lead to freedom. The Buddha, Socrates, and Jesus asked people to love each other unsentimentally, willing the best good for the other with compassionate awareness. If by luck and good will humanity survives and flourishes, the world will continue to see more and more millions of women and men who love each other so absolutely and who live, work, and raise children in many combinations.

Unmarried women, living alone or with roommates, with children or not, have dramatically changed the emotional landscape of middle-class life in the United States over the last thirty years. Flourishing at the edges of the patriarchy, these women often connect remarkably large and diverse networks of friends and relations. I have seen gatherings called into being by these women and wondered at the relatively narrow circle my wife and I live within. And while unmarried men remain the source of most crime and subject themselves disproportionately to suicide and substance abuse, unmarried women have moved into the center of the U.S. economy and popular culture. Television both enshrines and belittles Mary Richards, Murphy Brown, Ellen, and Ally McBeal as secular saints, models of pluck and integrity; but these women serve as a sign that the domestic religion is changing, and that the role of single women in formal religion and politics will also grow.

The United States now offers an ethic of freedom and the most unlimited field for the expression of love in the history of the world. Dangers inherent to the situation include the further dissolution of the family and the loss of knowledge that love means something different from intense feeling. Because freedom frightens people, some will flee into reactionary movements. Others may identify themselves with particular sexual practices, proclaiming their rights and displaying "the frozen countenance of the perversions" that Michel Foucault identified as one result of modern, medical investigations of sex.[13] Whether we use our freedom for true friendship or sink into self-indulgent sentimentality and compulsive pursuit of ecstasy depends on whether we can simultaneously liberate and discipline ourselves. People trying to combine liberation and discipline have often worked through prayer, which is one of the ways to strengthen the bond between spiritual and physical life.

EXERCISE, PRAYER,
AND MAGIC

· 9 ·

People who pray authentically or exercise mindfully will not go far wrong in any part of life. Although all prayer is exercise, not all exercise is prayer; nor is all prayer authentic or all exercise mindfully done. Many people seek magic—inexplicable forces and sympathies of matter and energy—not only in prayer and in exercise, but also in science, especially physics and medicine. Some rush to encounters with dangerous forces, while others seek less than they could.

In the United States today, about 90 percent of adults say that they pray and a quarter exercise regularly;[1] many are driven by addictions either to one or to both. The same reluctance to admit our need to alter our moods that distorts the debate about substances also inhibits discussion of what people want and what they do when they pray and exercise. Even more intense inhibitions arise with regard to prayer and exercise than with regard to drugs, because attitudes toward exercise, prayer, and magic are often learned in childhood and never examined by adults. Reflection may open new ways to freedom, techniques for practice, and glimpses of the truths behind powerful emotions.

Victorian distrust of the body, Christian petitions of God, and rationalist dismissals of magic still flourish in

The collective conscience about exercise, prayer, and magic has long been moving from West to East.

the United States. Meanwhile, counter-currents toward enjoying exercise, meditating rather than petitioning, and accepting magical practices run through the culture. The wife of a rabbi has for years been the best-known yoga teacher in my area. Eclectic books such as Mirka Knaster's *Discovering the Body's Wisdom*, which brings together exercises in everything from tai chi chuan to Rolfing on pages studded with boxed quotes from ancient and modern gurus, have become as normal as videotapes on rock-hard abdominal muscles. The collective conscience about exercise, prayer, and magic has long been moving from West to East, from Protestant to Catholic, and from Judeo-Christian to what our ancestors would have called pagan and native (including European witchcraft and African and Native American healing techniques); but our historical perspectives and theoretical frames have not kept pace. Even if we are no more physically fit or spiritually aware than fifty years ago, the paths down which we pursue these goals have dramatically broadened.

It seems certain that more amateur athletes and exercise addicts run and treadmill and StairMaster through life in the United States than through any society in history. Only thirty years ago, anyone who ran in the streets of a city or town attracted the derision of children and the pursuit of dogs. To run in the 1960s broke the peace; police looked suspiciously on runners. In 1977, running guru Jim Fixx signaled a change when he put the quote "A good run makes you feel sort of holy" on the first page of *The Complete Book of Running*.[2] Now twenty thousand marathoners—people so well trained that they can run for twenty-six miles—swarm across the Verrazano Bridge and through the streets of New York City every November. Some future generation will almost certainly find this behavior as bizarre as modern people find the bands of penitents, called flagellants, who went from town to town whipping each other and praying during plague years in the Middle Ages. But the crowds massed for a road race are not doing penance; at least at the starting line, they are giddy with camaraderie, buoyed on a sea of self-transcendence.

The relation between running and meditation should be clear to anyone who has done both. With the first strides of a solitary run, the combination of a few deep breaths and the knowledge that three miles of road or ten miles of crushed gravel in a park lie ahead make the heart race and lead to a high, a rush of oxygen and adrenaline. The mind opens to grand ideas. After a rhythm of breathing and striding sets in, ecstatic thinking—a state of being beside oneself in thought—may elaborate an inspiration or fix on a source of worry. Endorphins flow, offering support for several kinds of consciousness. Physical feelings conducive to purgation and illumination, the first two steps in classical Western descriptions of spiritual life, happen automatically, perhaps accompanied by the spiritual acts of self-critical thinking and acceptance of joy in the moment. Behind these states of mind comes a sense of mastery, of running beyond slavery to reflex and sentiment. The runner may feel emotion more poignantly, but the discipline of running provides choices of attitude regarding that emotion. By entering an extreme physical state, the runner gives freedom to the mind.

The term *ascetic,* denoting those who renounce the world to devote themselves to prayer, comes from the Greek *ascesis,* exercise. Ignatius of Loyola, the founder of the Jesuit order of priests, called his instructions for meditation *Spiritual Exercises.* In these guided meditations, Ignatius told his followers to use and to develop the faculties of memory, reason, and will; all meditation in the school of St. Ignatius aims to inform and to strengthen acts of will.[3] The beginning runner is without question ascetic. To keep running after only a hundred yards, beyond the anaerobic paces that one could take holding one's breath to the point where it becomes necessary to breathe hard, already demands an act of will. To finish a common road race of three to five miles, let alone a marathon of twenty-six, involves resisting the desire to quit, choosing discomfort in service of a goal.

Since Socrates and Plato, and especially since Aristotle's *Ethics,* moralists have used physical exercise as a model for character development. Aristotle valued difficulty for its own sake, describing human nature as a board that needed force to bend it into shape.[4] Just as a board can be bent by several kinds of tools, so a person can be trained by several kinds of exercise; and the feelings of those exercising may change as they approach their goal. Practices such as running, swimming, and aerobics bring the whole body into play, mov-

The relation between running and meditation should be clear.

Although all prayer is exercise, not all exercise is prayer.

ing the mind with the body, burning many calories, and stressing the heart and lungs directly. Exercises such as yoga and tai chi harmonize mind and body with breathing and posture to improve flexibility, circulation, and strength without forcing the heart, lungs, or muscles to become larger. Precision exercises such as ballet, modern dance, and Asian martial arts fill the body with awareness. Although bodybuilding with weights seems brutal and its results grotesque to many, it forms a subset of the precision exercises; intelligent weightlifters work with awareness of every movement and every muscle to promote an ideal shape.

The moods induced by aerobic, harmonic, and precision exercises seem naturally suitable to three kinds of prayer: aerobic exercise to prayers of petition and praise; harmonic exercise to prayers that induce meditative trance; and precision exercise to the simple practice of presence that is sometimes called contemplation. These three aspects of exercise and prayer correspond in turn to the stages of purgation, illumination, and union that Western writers of many centuries have described as phases of spiritual life.[5] A runner who has reached sufficient fitness and bodily consciousness may, however, run right through purgation, petition, and praise to meditation, to the inspired ideas and feelings of illumination, and on to calm awareness or union. Meanwhile, a ballet dancer having difficulties may not reach beyond purgation.

Not all exercise is prayer. Competitive runners often use a temporary trance not to seek the depths of being but to avoid the awareness of pain. They sink below the waves of discomfort from lungs and feet and legs and stomach, stopping the mind to let the body do its job, but return frequently to consciousness to check their time or their position relative to others in the race. Competitive swimmers also use trance in this way, and many competitive runners and swimmers tend to have simple melodies, voluntarily or involuntarily selected, running through their minds as they exercise. Such athletes do not open their exercise to the religious dimension except perhaps by praying before or after competition.

Functional trances also appeal to some of the noncompetitive runners, swimmers, cyclists, users of exercise machines, and members of aerobics or step classes who become addicted to aerobic exercise, often neglecting family and work and other forms of recreation. These people may work out with other people and enter road races, approaching through their fidelity the social commitment appropriate to religion. The endorphin rush forms a large part of what addicts them, but they do not use the endorphin high for meditative thinking or prayer; a spiritual teacher might say that they are stuck in the stage of purgation, especially if they feel guilty when they do not work out. Their exercise itself opens no doors of awareness.

Whether we use physical exercise for prayer or not, anyone who prays outside a service of worship needs a ritual that clears the mind of daily cares and internal chatter. Only after entering a liminal state can we deeply will some good for ourselves or others, realize the humble place humanity has in the world and seek some higher power, or simply acknowledge the wonder of being.

For years, I shared the scorn that many people, including some believers, feel for prayers of petition. Why ask an omniscient God for anything, when God should already know what we need? With all the suffering and injustice in the world, who are we wealthy people in the United States to ask for anything? When constructing a midterm test for a course in Catholic theology, I assigned my students to comment on several statements, including this: "Prayer reflects a childish belief in the omnipotence of wishes." One good answer I imagined would have admitted that petitionary prayer often did reflect such illusions, but that meditative or contemplative prayer could also serve higher goals of spiritual development.

Then I invited Sister Cora Brady, a former professor of religion and dean of the faculty at Manhattanville, to teach a session of the class. I watched in amazement as this tall, ethereally thin woman in her seventies sat down and spoke so quietly and precisely that she turned a lecture hall seating a hundred into a parlor where she communicated intimately with two or three dozen widely scattered students. Regarding the statement about prayer, Brady said that the omnipotence of wishes was not just a childish belief. "What is more powerful or more important than what one wishes?" she asked. I was forced to reflect on the relation of petitionary prayer to her presence in

> What is more important than what one wishes?

Petitionary prayer

entails a kind of test: does

that goal matter enough

to pray for it?

my class, despite her original opposition to my appointment on the grounds that I wrote too much about sex. I prayed very hard for the Manhattanville job—the only time I ever prayed for a job—in a five-hour drive after my interview.

We often worry that we will not get what we want, but rarely consider what will happen if we do. This attitude holds dangers, especially among educated and wealthy people who usually manage to get what they want. Petitionary prayer entails a kind of test: does that goal matter enough to pray for it? Is it a desire that should be entertained at all? If you cannot pray for something, should you want it? Prayers of petition can remind us to take care that we choose what we want.

In the classic Christian prayer of petition, often called the Lord's Prayer, the Our Father, or the Prayer of Jesus, billions of people for thousands of years have prayed for the end of the world. "Thy kingdom come," they say every day, in churches everywhere. Even the prayer for "daily bread" refers to the return of daily manna from heaven, the bread that the Israelites received in the Exodus, and that should come again with the Messiah. The petition to "lead us not into temptation, but deliver us from evil," is sometimes translated with reference to "the Evil One"; it relates to the final contest of God and Satan. Such requests, even when their meaning lingers at the threshold of consciousness, shape everyday Christian attitudes. These petitions encourage Christians to reject the present condition of the world and nurture a sense of imminent crisis and danger.

A similar mood occurs in the second greatest Christian prayer, used by a billion Roman Catholics, the Hail Mary. "Pray for us, now and at the hour of our death," that prayer concludes, reminding everyone of mortality. But the Our Father and the Hail Mary also work very differently. The prayer ascribed to Jesus is a complex set of requests, each of which demands attention; the Hail Mary simply calls up an image, the image of Mary, the Blessed Mother, and asks her to pray to God on behalf of humanity. Saying the Prayer of Jesus without thinking about the words seems degrading, but the Hail Mary serves, without demanding thought, as a vehicle for fixing the mind on a single image and a single mood. Repetitions of the Hail

Mary form most of the substance of the rosary, a meditation long prescribed for everyday use by the Roman Catholic Church.

Rosaries look superstitious to Protestants, and even among Catholics the rosary often falls under the critical assessment that a little education or a little religious experience leads people to make of "rote" or "mechanical" prayer, by which they mean repetition without reflection upon meaning. Such criticisms reveal a concept of prayer that omits the traditional use of circles of beads and spinning motions to induce trance. Within these trances, apparently mindless repetition can support vast networks of meaning and intense emotional energies. Mechanical prayer also has the advantage that, requiring no inspiration to begin, it can become a reliable way to invite inspiration every day.

Consider the details of how the rosary works. Around the circle, five sets of ten beads are separated by four empty stretches of chain, in the middle of which sit single beads. Where the fifth single bead would be, a short piece of chain, ending in a crucifix, attaches; because of the cross under the circle, a whole rosary resembles the modern symbol for woman used in medicine and the feminist movement. The short chain contains five beads, three set close together in the middle and one isolated near each end. A medal or cameo of the Virgin Mary, the woman Catholics call the "mother of God," marks the place where the short chain attaches to the circle.

Praying the rosary, whether in private or in unison, involves fifty-three repetitions of the Hail Mary, the text of which combines the salutations of the Virgin by the angel Gabriel and Elizabeth in the Gospel of Luke: "Hail Mary, full of grace, the Lord is with thee. Blessed art thou among women, and blessed is the fruit of thy womb, Jesus." Then the one, completely empty petition: "Holy Mary, Mother of God, pray for us sinners, now and at the hour of our death." Although these words connect with great themes of theology—including the doctrine of original sin, that makes all people into "us sinners"; the title "Mother of God," which the Council of Ephesus gave to Mary in 341; and whatever implications may be read into "Holy Mary," which might extend to the idea that Mary herself was conceived without sin—the prayer does not di-

Apparently mindless repetition can support networks of meaning and intense energies.

The rosary provides

a way into trance and

much more: a connection

with spiritual power.

rect the mind to these themes. Brief and without petitions of its own, the Hail Mary is ideally suited to carry other ideas.

This is exactly how the church prescribes that the Hail Mary be used in a rosary. While saying ten Hail Marys, those who pray are instructed to think not about the words but about events in the lives (and afterlives) of Jesus and Mary. These events are organized according to days of the week. On Mondays and Thursdays, the prescribed subjects for meditation are the Joyful Mysteries: with the first ten Hail Marys, one thinks of the Annunciation. Gabriel asks Mary to bear the Child—a request, and not a rape, unlike the relations of Zeus with human women. The second decade belongs to the Visitation: Mary visits her cousin Elizabeth, then pregnant with John the Baptist; John leaps in Elizabeth's womb, and Elizabeth says that Mary is "blessed among women"; Mary delivers prophetic praise of God and denunciation of the wealthy and powerful in the Magnificat. With the third set of ten Hail Marys, worshipers think of the Nativity; with the fourth, the Circumcision of Jesus (celebrated on January 1, following Jewish law on the eighth day after the birth, but now called the Presentation at the Temple to protect Gentile sensitivities); and with the fifth decade, attention turns to the recovery of Jesus at twelve years old, when he was found arguing with the priests of the Temple, after Mary and Joseph had lost him on their Passover visit to Jerusalem.

Of course, no one could think of such complex themes and the words of an unrelated prayer at the same time. But to use the rosary most effectively, one should go further and apply the meditations to one's own life. For example, the decade of the Nativity leads me to give thanks for my wife's safe delivery of our son; the decade on finding Jesus teaching in the Temple leads me to pray for my son's education. While meditating on the circumcision of Jesus, I often hope for more male students to enroll in our predominantly female college.

Such meditations require that the prayer itself take no mental energy, but serve as a mantra to keep the mind clear and focused. In public, if a group recites the rosary, the leader says the first part in one breath: "HailMaryfullofgracetheLORDiswiththee;blessedartTHOU amongwomenandblessedisthefruitofTHYwombJesus." Then the people reply, also in one breath: "HolyMaryMotherofGodprayforus sinnersNOWandatthehourofourdeathamen." Replicating this in private taught me how to say the rosary by myself. Whenever fifteen minutes become available, most often in my automobile commute or on a long run (where ten fingers can substitute for the ten beads in each decade), the rosary provides a way into trance and much more: a connection with spiritual power that has at least whatever metaphysical status may belong to deep emotion. On the most unverifiable but crucial side of my own experience, I feel sure that the rosary has connected with two miracles in my life.

Willingness to accept spiritual effects in the physical world, and even to pray for them, represents an increasingly strong aspect of our domestic religion. To some degree all prayer, including the Psalms and the Buddhist and Muslim and Greek Christian rosaries, implies a hope for miracles. But the Roman Catholic rosary, made up of prayers to Mary, turns the attitude of petitioning a father for benefits into a posture of hopefully expecting good things from a mother. The Catholic rosary contains approaches to the body, the physical world, and the life of the spirit that can look surprisingly compatible with modern feminism and with the Gaia hypothesis, in which the world itself is a living spirit.

For example, the fourth and fifth decades of the Glorious Mysteries, said on Sundays, Wednesdays, and Saturdays, are devoted to the Assumption of Mary into heaven and the crowning of Mary as Queen of Heaven. The Assumption—involving a transformation of Mary's body into one like the glorified, resurrected body of Jesus—was proclaimed a dogma of the Catholic Church by Pope Pius XII in 1950, in the only papal pronouncement that has ever explicitly claimed an infallible revelation by the Holy Spirit. Writing in the early 1950s, Carl Jung reflected that the proclamation of this doctrine represented the acceptance of the human body as sacred and a sign that women would attain equality with men in the church and the world.[6] As for the status of Mary as Queen of Heaven, Jung pointed out that this made the Trinity into a Quaternity, or, as I was taught in catechism, that

> Jung reflected that the Assumption represented acceptance of the body.

The moods of the Psalms range from bitter repentance to solemn joy to exultation in violence.

Mary as Mother of God rules all creatures. Neither the Temple nor any other place on earth could contain God, but Mary's womb did, and since then God remains in the world, nourishing us in bread and wine. The curve of the sky has become the womb of the world.

The beginning and end of the rosary exemplify this move from patriarchy to matriarchy. While holding the crucifix at the beginning, one recites the Apostles' Creed, a story full of the "Father" and the "Son," who is shown as a hero who comes down from heaven and even descends into hell to save us. But after the circuit of five decades, when the rosary ends, one emerges from whatever mood or trance the chant has induced by way of a prayer called the Salve Regina and recited on the cameo of Mary: "Hail, holy Queen, Mother of mercy; hail our life, our sweetness and our hope. To thee do we cry, poor banished children of Eve; to thee do we send up our sighs, mourning and weeping in this valley of tears. Turn then, O most gracious advocate, thine eyes of truth upon us, and after this our exile, show unto us the blessed fruit of thy womb, Jesus. O clement, O loving, O sweet virgin Mary, Queen of the most Holy Rosary, pray for us." Where the creed dwells on heroism and triumph, the Salve Regina exalts submission and the expectation of suffering. Where the creed asserts, the Salve Regina requests, even begs.

For about fifteen years, I balanced occasional use of the rosary (in crisis, but without the frequent opportunity offered by a long commute) with morning and evening reading of the Psalms, in the Miles Coverdale translation that appears, divided into a thirty-day circuit, in the Episcopal Book of Common Prayer. The moods of the Psalms range from bitter repentance to solemn joy to exultation in violence: "I will follow upon mine enemies, and overtake them; . . . I will beat them as small as the dust before the wind, I will cast them out as the clay in the streets" (Ps. 18:37, 42). These poems reflect, according to tradition, the violent life of King David, the first author of Psalms. Even in more reflective moods, their symbols are as male as the rosary's are female.

For deliverance from the storms of Christian and Jewish struggles with God and with each other, the possibilities of daily prayer include the simple, Buddhist rosary, consisting of one hundred and eight wooden beads, exactly twice as many as the Christian circle; one bead for each of the desires to be renounced so that suffering will cease. All the Buddhist beads are identical, and the same distance apart, except for a crystal bead to mark the middle and a larger crystal with the rope of the rosary passing through it to mark the beginning and end. On each bead I chant the same thing: "Gate, gate [pronounced *gahteh, gahteh*], paragate, parasamgate, Bodhi, svaha;" which means, "Gone, gone, altogether gone, altogether completely gone, Awareness, hail." What is gone, on the first level of meaning, is the historic Buddha. The chant asserts that he has really, altogether and completely, left the cycle of rebirths fueled by desire, and the concluding phrase hails the naked awareness, the simplicity of compassion, that enabled the Buddha, who began his last earthly life as the man Siddhartha Gautama, to become free. On the level of practice these words, which have their rhythm in themselves, gain their meaning only as they are chanted, calming the mind's turbulence. Chanting, one can see that we ourselves will be gone, gone, altogether gone, altogether completely gone; that we need not worry that the world will not go on without us; that we also can freely dissolve into pure compassionate awareness.

Though all rosaries use repetition to lower the barriers of self so that people can sense a more general power, the differences between religions still matter. The Muslim orders of mystics known (for their plain woolen clothing) as the Sufis use a rosary with large beads, on which they chant the usual opening of Islamic prayer, the blessing of God that begins the Qur'an, followed by many repetitions of the name of Allah. The Orthodox Christians of Greece and Russia use a simple circle of beads for the "Jesus prayer," which is the basic practice of the mystics called Hesychasts. "Lord Jesus, save me, a sinner," they repeat on each bead, and their circle has no marker for stopping; they want to continue praying until the prayer says itself through them. These rosaries illustrate a characteristic difference between Muslims and Christians and a common limitation of theistic prayer. Muslims, like Jews, often make praise of God the only subject of their

Buddhism cuts directly through the dualistic problem by denying that any God exists.

Muslims praise God;

Jews seek union with God

in practice.

prayers. The Greek "Jesus prayer" praises Jesus by calling him "Lord," but primarily concerns the sinful self and its need for salvation. The Muslim rosary is a prayer of praise, the Christian a prayer of petition. By either vehicle, people can move through purgation into illumination. The limitation that both prayers have in common arises from the essences of praise and petition, both of which presume a distance between subject and object that would seem to prevent going beyond illumination into union. Many think that union with God must be possible because, if God is real, God must be here as well as everywhere else, acting in all things, closer (as the Muslims say) than the vein in your neck. Yet, prayers of praise and petition both seem to reinforce an image of God on a throne, separate and distant from us, and finite—one member of a subject-object pair.

Jews have generally remained content with this division, engaging in millennia of dialogue with God that has included not only praise and petition, but also much recrimination and argument. According to one of the most prominent Jewish thinkers of the twentieth century, Martin Buber, dialogue is the only possible way for a human to approach God. Being infinite, God can never be an object, wrote Buber in his classic *I and Thou;* only a word of address, a "Thou" spoken from the whole heart, connects the human and the divine. Attempts to dissolve this dialogue into a spiritual or materialistic monism struck Buber as evasions of relationship.[7] His judgment continued a Jewish tradition expressed in one of the tales of the founder of Hasidism, the rabbi known as the Baal Shem Tov, who was said to have been about to enter unity with God when his wife's voice called him back.[8] Although the Torah can be read for messages about the nature of God, and some love mysticism can be found in later writings such as the Song of Songs or passages in the prophets, the Hebrew Scriptures contain no directions for seeking union with God.

Perhaps Judaism emphasizes the prayer of union less because Jews seek union with God in practice. While a Catholic may say the rosary every day and an Orthodox Christian or a Sufi Muslim might try to pray constantly, the genius of Judaism lies in sanctifying every action of everyday life. Kosher laws make every meal a religious event; the

Sabbath rest centers every week; passing through any doorway involves touching its *mezuzah,* a case containing the words that God is one; the sacredness of blood limits all physical contact between husbands and wives to about two weeks a month. In short, the Torah has 613 laws which amount to so many ways to make every action religious, and the traditions of Talmud and continuing *responsa* add thousands more. For a believing Jew, oneness with God extends even beyond these, because every fact of apparently profane history and politics really has its place in the journey of history toward the Messianic age, when all nations will know the God of Israel.

Buddhism cuts directly through the dualistic problem by denying that any God exists. And in literal truth, God cannot exist, because to exist derives from *ex* and *sto,* the Latin for "I stand"—to exist is to stand out. We can tell that we exist, and that other objects in the world exist, because we can stand on a scale holding the object, then put it down and determine our separate weights. With God, we can never do this; and as I told my son when he asked why God is invisible, any real God would be too big to see. If there is a God, God simply is. It may be better not to discuss God or gods, because discourse inevitably reduces God to an object. Perhaps this wisdom underlies the Torah's prohibition on saying the name of God, a law that still leads many Jews to write G-d instead of God.

To encounter being directly, as some Buddhists teach, just sit down and pay attention. Stop thinking about God; if God were trying to speak to you now, how would you know unless you listen? Spend some time awake and aware but thinking of nothing, and find that being reveals itself. Pick a place with plain uncluttered space in front of you; set an alarm for twenty minutes, sit down, and don't move. Use the floor and the lotus position (because it is most stable) if you can, but sitting works in any position that you can hold comfortably. Keep your eyes open but look at nothing; focus gently on a spot a few feet away, with your gaze cast down. A floor of indefinite patterns, such as sand or the nubbles of industrial carpeting, works well. Breathe regularly and fully; some people count breaths, but that seems counterproductive to me. Do not force yourself to think of anything or of nothing. Thoughts will come, but

> To encounter being directly just sit down and pay attention.

Yoga and tai chi unify exercise and religion.

just sit and refuse to follow them; let them come and pass, as though they were leaves in a river flowing by. If a noise happens, let it wash over you and let it go. Wait for no fireworks or special effects; the practice itself is the answer. You may begin to see as a baby sees, with completely open eyes and no presuppositions or judgments to block perception. For those who see in this way, God is here—if you still need or want to use that name.

I have heard that school days in Japan often begin with fifteen minutes of sitting. In my college classrooms in the United States, five minutes drives some people crazy. Only twenty minutes a day for a couple of months gave me the assurance that even if I lose my memory before I die, as my father did from Alzheimer's in his eighties, arriving at a point where he no longer remembered me, things would still be all right. The world does not depend on my thinking.

For every person intrigued by simple sitting, dozens are drawn to the specific breathing and posture and exercise techniques of the Hindu approach to meditation, yoga. Yoga simply means discipline; the word has the same root as "yoke" and contains the idea of union. Always beginning with an awareness of breath and proceeding through various bodily positions (*asanas*) and sounds (*mantras*), in Hindu tradition yoga serves many purposes, from improving posture and flexibility to impressing people with physical tricks like nearly stopping the heart or lying on nails to seeking freedom from the round of rebirths. We often use yoga only to improve flexibility and relaxation, but we may find in it the intersection of exercise and prayer.

Packaging a more accessible yoga for the United States, the Maharishi Mahesh Yogi scored a notable success with transcendental meditation or TM because he pitched the ancient wisdom in terms of specific benefits: lowered heart rates, lowered blood pressure, better sleep, more success in the world. At the higher levels of TM (which has practically become a formal religion, with a university in Iowa for training leaders), people claim to levitate, and groups of TM practitioners gather and meditate in order to lower the crime rates of cities and to bring about world peace.

From China, the United States receives disciplines and teachings that focus neither on the breath, as in yoga, nor the mind, as in Zen, but more broadly on the *chi*—the life force that works through everything that is. While mountains cannot sit zazen or do yoga, the *chi* of mountains can certainly be felt in a landscape by a skillful painter who has sat and absorbed that force, then returned to the studio to express it. The movements of exercise called tai chi, which can be seen at dawn in any Chinese neighborhood in the world, with no two people moving in the same way but all following traditional patterns, adjusting for the flow of *chi* in the particular person, unify the realms of physical exercise and religion as certainly as Indian yoga. For those who inherit, continue, and transmit the discipline of tai chi, the world does not move as a machine; it dances.

Two or three decades ago, both practitioners and opponents of non-Western ways of exercise, prayer, and meditation would have seen them as examples of magical thinking, requiring a complete shift of metaphysical perspective, a denial of Western concepts of matter and life, cause and effect. These methods do not seem so exotic today because our minds have opened to magic.

When Arthur Miller wrote his play on the 1691 Salem witch trials, *The Crucible,* the audiences of the 1950s knew for certain that there were no real witches, in Salem or anywhere else, and that the real subject of the play was the dynamic of suspicion and accusation revealed in the cold war, and especially in Senator Joseph McCarthy's campaign against Communist infiltrators. The term *witch hunt* still means a persecution based on unsubstantiated suspicions and nonexistent crimes.

But in the 1990s, many women in Salem, Massachusetts, and elsewhere proudly claim the name of witches. A coven dances under every full moon on the beach at West Haven, Connecticut, less than ten miles from where I now sit. At the World Parliament of Religions in Chicago in 1993, I visited a booth run by a national organization of witches, the Covenant of the Goddess, which stood alphabetically next to the booth representing the Boy Scouts of America. A friendly Texan at the Boy Scout booth told the witches that his national office would authorize a merit badge in witchcraft, just as the scouts have approved badges for Muslim and Catholic activities, if the Covenant of the Goddess managed to sponsor as many as fourteen troops of scouts.

In the 1990s, many women proudly claim the name of witches.

Our minds have

opened to magic.

In the 1980 campaign for the Republican presidential nomination, George Bush hung the label of "voodoo economics" on Ronald Reagan's supply-side hope that cutting taxes would increase tax revenues because of increased economic activity; *voodoo* then meant an unfounded and magical system of beliefs and practices. Today, we know voodoo, *santeria,* and *condomblé* as American names for a religious tradition from West Africa, and to use "voodoo" to denote falsity insults both the Yoruba and Fon peoples of Nigeria and Dahomey and millions of African Americans in Haiti, Cuba, Brazil, and the United States. The connections of voodoo with other U.S. religions, especially Pentecostal Christianity, have been explored by Albert Raboteau in *Slave Religion* and Joseph Murphy in *Working the Spirit;* Harvard professor Karen McCarthy Brown has written of her initiation into a Brooklyn voodoo family in *Mama Lola;* and the pioneering documentary film made by Maya Deren, *Divine Horsemen,* has been joined by a respectful two-hour television special on voodoo, hosted by Leonard Nimoy, from the Arts & Entertainment cable television network.

Protests against the rise of magic in the United States come from evangelical Christians, from cultural conservatives, and from some scientists. Under evangelical pressure, celebrations of Halloween have been banned at many public schools, even as Halloween celebrations grow longer and more elaborate in other school systems. Conservatives rail at popular fantasies such as "Dungeons and Dragons" and the card game called "Magic: The Gathering," which has been used to teach arithmetic. Scientists sometimes decry the readiness of the public to accept alternative medicine, spiritual healing, and mystical perspectives on physics.

For most of the neoorthodox, Protestant-oriented thinkers who long dominated U.S. scholarship on religion, magic had a negative connotation. Martin Buber, in *I and Thou,* summed up the argument when he wrote that prayer and magic were qualitatively different, because those who maintained an attitude of prayer sought relationship first, then effects, while the believer in magic sought the effects first, and might not be interested in addressing or relating to or receiving from God at all. For years I shared, and uncritically taught, Buber's distinction between prayer and magic. It still seems to have some validity, and the distinction offers the comfort (for a believer) of classifying magic not as primitive religion but as primitive science or technology, an early attempt to manipulate the world objectively, by knowledge and force. Authentic religion, in ancient times or today, would always have the qualitatively different aim of entering into relationship.

In our eagerness to defend religion and rationalism, we were overlooking what Jungian psychology calls the mechanism of compensation. The mind needs and craves balance. As the formal religions become more rational and less distinct from one another, the domestic religion grows more colorful and magical. If Roman Catholics taught their children all of their church's traditions about the ranks of angels, the levels of heaven and hell, and the powers of saints over particular aspects of the world, Catholic children would have no need for the powerful creatures and spells depicted on Magic cards. And in another form of compensation, magic adds personality and a sense of contact to a world in which medicine, politics, and economics can seem increasingly baffling and impersonal. The collective conscience that Emile Durkheim expected to see in any unified economic system remained strong in the United States through the 1960s; but since then, international business has developed such coercive power and hidden its real structure and aims so completely that the atmosphere Durkheim called anomie prevails. Who takes the speeches of the corporate CEO or the president of the United States at face value? In the age of health maintenance organizations, profit-making hospitals, and plagues from other countries, how can we trust our doctors? Magic not only gives its practitioners a sense of power; the magical worldview can reinforce belief in God by making a place for personality among the powers of the world. Even those who have no access to the Force themselves may be glad to see Luke Skywalker of *Star Wars* using it. When priests and doctors cannot tell us how to secure places in heaven or on earth, it may be reassuring to call home with E.T.

The distinction between magic and prayer began to break down for me in 1993, when I attended the World Parliament of Religions in Chicago and heard voodoo priests speak for themselves. When people pray for the spirit of an animal being sacrificed so that a spirit may possess a priest who will then take part in a

Magic adds personality

and a sense of contrast.

Everything can be
described as energy.

healing ritual, are they simply trying to manipulate the world by force? No more than millions of other people in the United States, who often seek tangible effects from prayer. On the 700 Club and in Christian Science, on thousands of cable channels and in thousands of churches, people lay claims on healings, guidance, even prosperity through spiritual power. Pentecostal Christians pray over every decision; one told me that he "dispatched angels to the north, west, east, and south" to find buyers for his father's house. For him, prayer that seeks no effects seems suspect, as though non-Pentecostals refuse to connect with divine power because they want to continue believing in human autonomy. While Pentecostals would condemn the witches I saw in Chicago, calling on the powers of elements instead of angels as they face the directions, both Pentecostals and witches testify that real relationships involve real energies.

Even one so intolerant of magic as Martin Buber wrote that an artist, as opposed to a technician, spoke the word of address to a tree that would serve as subject of a painting.[9] Those who seek healing with the laying on of hands, with herbs gathered at the equinox, or with possession and trance may be authentically praying, entering into relationship with the divine in Buber's terms; it may be those who sprinkle holy water on the metal coffin or carry the Torah around the synagogue who sink into the lower attitude of purely instrumental, superstitious magic. Attitudes remain intangible, unknowable from outside.

If we can judge by results ("You will know them by their fruits," as Jesus says in Matthew 7:16), a great deal of bad magic presently works in the domestic religion. Millions flock to houses of worship—churches and synagogues, temples and mosques and revival meetings—and emerge narrower and more negative, denouncing presidents and social programs, clutching slogans and reflexive answers that prevent thought. Millions waste their hours sweating on stair machines, foolishly supporting their weight on the railings, or stride along treadmills while they grow a little heavier each month. And as we read newspaper horoscopes, consult psychic friends at 900 numbers, play the state lotteries, and hang mass-produced "Native American" dreamcatchers above our children's beds, we may need to reflect on the evangelical slogan that people who have no faith will believe anything.

Meanwhile, the last thirty years have seen some undeniably positive spiritual development. Voodoo, witchcraft, and Native American religions have risen from neglect and scorn to respect among scholars and seekers. Those thousands of runners in our marathons represent an achievement, a gathering of mystics, as well as a spectacle that rivals the medieval flagellants. A common concept of energy, the intellectual by-product of modern physics, informs much of the discourse about exercise, prayer, and magic from Jim Fixx's books on running to *The Celestine Prophecy*. Having learned that everything from the quark and the electron to the stars can be described as energy at various quantum levels, many have opened their minds to the Chinese *chi* and Indian *kundalini,* the *mana* of Pacific islanders, and the *orenda* and *wakantanka* of Native Americans, the healing and dangerous forces that biblical peoples called holiness and power and glory. Although I could not sacrifice an animal myself, I can begin to grasp what voodoo priests mean when they say that sacrifice releases energy. Quantum physics leads to speculation about the energy fields of human minds, and therefore about telekinesis, extrasensory perception, prophecy, reincarnation, and other effects Einstein tried to dismiss as "spooky action at a distance."

In the classic *Religion and the Decline of Magic,* Keith Thomas argued that the late-medieval Lollards and early Protestants gave up magical beliefs on religious grounds even before they had any scientific or technical replacements, and therefore that these religious movements prepared the modern mind to accept rationalist, quantifiable science.[10] Now, ironically, science disposes people to accept magic. Some of the most magical texts in the bookstores, books dealing with immortality, healing, and hidden powers of matter and spirit, are written by physicists and physicians. Out of the most extreme developments of modern rationality, discipline, and independence emerge postmodern versions of magic, exercise, and prayer.

Our attempts to manipulate energy express the need we feel to find a new harmony with nature. The next chapter describes how seasons and stages of life gain power and history recedes in the domestic religion even as technology makes people seem independent of time.

· IO ·   SEASONS

Just as without faith, people will believe anything, so those who lack real connections to nature fall prey to unconscious domination by seasons and directions, stages and cycles. All the neopagans in the United States do not dance around fires in covens; in fact, the cults of Christmas, Hanukkah, and Halloween have made most of us neopagans. If we remember that "pagan" is related to *paisan* and originally meant country people as opposed to urbanites, the persistence of paganism should become less alarming. Considering how the seasons work in our domestic religion may help us to anticipate the flow of time and to ride the seasonal energies, both through the year and through life.

When I ask my students what phase the moon is in, or where it will rise tonight, no one knows; if the moon is full a few may have noticed. I don't usually know myself. But I ask the question to show how alienated we are from facts of nature that would have been known to all of our ancestors from time immemorial. Even in a classroom where late afternoon light streams through the windows, a majority of my college students do not know which direction is west.

Before electric light, central heat, and the idols of the movies, television, and virtual reality, the moon meant light or darkness, the ability to see well enough to move around safely after sunset or not. The stars were a carpet of fire overhead, the most entertaining thing visible at night, with patterns that repeated themselves as the year turned. Besides providing light, the stars showed the time to plant corn in America or wheat in Europe or rice in Asia. Every culture had an astrology, not simply because people saw lions or archers in the stars but because they knew that the position of the stars gave valuable knowledge about what time of year it was, how much light there would be, and what the weather would be like, all of which related to what moods would be common among people. If we returned in a time machine to any of the centuries before our own, we would seem unbelievably ignorant about the time of day, the seasons, the compass directions, and the likely locations of food and water.

Still, the seasons pull on us, perhaps even more strongly because we do not understand them. Of course, commercial interests exploit seasons, but these corporations and advertisers are only young parasites on the world's body, far too young to have produced mood shifts of this depth. Responses to the transformations of June and December, March and September must have long ago been bred into our bones. As evolutionary theorists might say, in the very long run the descendants of mammals who reacted correctly to these changes of light and weather have survived, and the line of those who responded inappropriately has died out. Small advantages acting over millions of years make large differences.

Objectively, the hours of daylight grow shorter until the winter solstice, then longer until the summer; one day in spring and one in fall see equal portions of sunshine and darkness. The differences are larger in the north; temperature and precipitation vary wildly because of local features like lakes, or on one side or the other of mountains; but nowhere in the United States lies so near the equator that the days remain the same length all year round.

To live through Christmas in this country is to feel the imperative power of the cycle. Most retail stores do half their business for the year in the month before Christmas. From the standpoint of an abstract standard of pure Christianity, such as the Puritans used, this represents a disaster of commercialism; but from the standpoint of the history of religions, all this buying and selling rightly responds to the rebirth of the world. When the sun darkens, then begins to strengthen again, the order of the world has to be reestablished. Identities and af-

The cults of Christmas, Hanukkah, and Halloween have made most of us neopagans.

filiations need to be defined by choosing and receiving gifts, and communities need to be reaffirmed by feasting. The darker and colder the world becomes at midwinter, the more vital this holiday is. And like all holidays, the midwinter holiday grows more important when the bonds of ordinary family life weaken.

People in the United States continue to spend time and money on Christmas even if their Christian belief and practice cease. They do not necessarily deserve to be seen as thoughtless materialists or condemned as hypocritical, because the midwinter festival draws on roots deep in pre-Christian days. Since Rome lies at the same latitude as New York, the weakening and strengthening of sunlight mattered enough so that Rome held a major festival, the birthday of the Unconquered Sun, at the winter solstice. With no biblical evidence for when Jesus was born, Christians baptized that Roman day as Christmas.

When the barbarians of northern Europe became Christian, they added new dimensions of ritual, such as Christmas trees, Yule logs, and the revelry of New Year's Eve. If all the day's light were an hour or so of twilight, and there had been less light every day for six months, imagine how important it might be when the sun began to grow stronger. The Yule log, burning through the crucial longest night, stands for the sun. Our Christmas tree is Yggdrasil, the World Tree of Norse mythology.[1] Its roots go into Hel, the abode of the dead; at the top sits Asgard, where the gods and heroes live. On the branches hang the stars and planets, including our own Midgard, home of mortals. Someday the whole tree will die, perhaps to rise again; but every winter we celebrate its return from dormancy for another season of light. If we set presents below the tree, with small statues of a mother and child and kings bearing gifts, we only add what the holy man Francis (St. Francis of Assisi) taught to make the tree Christian after the year 1200—more than a thousand years after the birth of the Jew that some thought was the Messiah.

Jews also have responded, especially in northern climates, to the power of midwinter. Though purists complain that Hanukkah began as a minor holiday with no tradition of gift-giving and that its growth in the United States reflects the need of assimilated Jews for a version of Christmas, Christmas and Hanukkah really respond to the same seasonal needs. Celebrating the rededication of the Jewish Temple after it had been profaned by Syrian-Greek overlords in the 160s B.C.E., the eight days of Hanukkah stand for a miracle in which lamp oil sufficient for one day burned in the Temple for eight. From the beginning, then, Hanukkah was a festival of light, placed on the calendar to fall near the winter solstice.

Drawing on the power of midwinter, in 1966 Dr. Maulana (formerly Ron) Karenga of the University of California created a holiday, Kwanzaa, now observed between December 26 and January 1 by thirteen million people in this country. Kwanzaa has taken a place next to Mother's Day as a holiday that has grown entirely in the domestic religion, originally without connections to formal religions or to the civil religion, although both Kwanzaa and Mother's Day have moved into many school systems and some churches. Like Hanukkah, a festival of light, Kwanzaa uses candles in a serious way: its candles march in order, three green on the left, three red on the right, and the *umoja* or Unity candle black at the center. Rather than celebrating a childbirth or a victory from the past, it seeks dedication to principles of action for the future. One of those principles, cooperative economics or commerce, attempts to deflect the commercialization of holidays toward economic action to benefit the African American community. And although Kwanzaa gifts are supposed to be handmade, the CNN Financial Network estimates that people spent five hundred million dollars celebrating the holiday in 1995.[2]

New Year's Day serves as a secular exit from our sacred time. Drink and debauchery, sophistication and noisemaking, crowds in Times Square and college football—on New Year's Eve and New Year's Day, the sacred season closes and profane time begins again. Without the preceding round of family dinners and visits and gift-giving, this depressurizing moment would have no meaning; but with the sacred duties done, another number can be added to the files and the checkbooks, and daily life can resume. New Year's Eve, especially as acted out for television in Times Square, where a chaotic mass of people watch

When the sun darkens, then begins to strengthen again, the order of the world has to be reestablished.

Our Christmas tree is

Yggdrasil, the World Tree

of Norse mythology

and are watched as they wait for a falling, symbolically shattering world in the form of a ball of light, completes the descent of the old year into the chaos of death so that a new year and a new order can be born.

Cultures and religions that developed closer to the equator often change years in the spring or (like Judaism) in the fall, with planting or harvest. Always the rites of the new year retain the sense of recreating the world. The prayers of Rosh Hashanah, the first day of the Jewish new year, invoke the creation, and eight days later Yom Kippur ends the autumn holiday with a sense that judgments for the new year have been made. But in a way Jews also start a year in spring, because the yearly cycle of the Torah readings begins again with Genesis at the holiday of Shavuot, called by the Greek name "Pentecost" in the Christian Scriptures, that falls seven weeks after Passover. Both Judaism and Christianity here retain some connection to the calendar that Abraham left behind in Babylon, where kings entered the abyss every spring and recreated the world.

Shadows of these spring and fall new years appear in the domestic religion of the United States through school calendars, with their increasingly important and numerous proms and homecomings, commencements and convocations, as well as in the openings of baseball and football seasons, the new collections of the fashion seasons, and new model years for automobiles. At the end of November, Thanksgiving stands at a powerful conjunction, serving both as the end of fall and as the first day of the dominant sacred season of midwinter.

Although Thanksgiving is proclaimed by the president and so begins in the civil religion before entering the domestic, the most important ways that people mark Thanksgiving pertain to the domestic side. No orthodoxy limits the rituals of this holiday, and no public ceremony, symbol, or monument has expressed it well enough to capture the imagination. When I informally survey my students, they tell me that turkey and sweet potatoes do not hold a mandatory or exclusive place at the Thanksgiving table. People bring whatever their families cook, adding the dishes together more or less wildly depending on how many ethnic groups connect with the hosts of the dinner. Always there are sacred dishes, however: the polenta in one family, the stuffed cabbage in another, the rice and beans or chorizo in a third and fourth. Pride links these multicultural expressions; people use their Thanksgiving dinners to eat symbols of what they affirm about themselves. While interfaith services often take place on or around Thanksgiving, the heart of the holiday is domestic, beating at the dinner table at home.

Spring comes a distant second to the midwinter sacred season in the United States, despite the serious attitude of official religion toward the holidays of Easter and Passover that take place at that time. And again in spring, the real power of these holidays comes not from the prophetic, historical religions of Abraham but from the cyclic, pagan, seasonal background. As Carl Jung reported decades ago, his Swiss compatriots often told him that they were not religious; then he would catch them hiding eggs and rabbit idols on their lawns. What did they mean by such rituals?[3] Mother's Day, although invented in Methodist Sunday schools and developed by florists and greeting card companies,[4] has ridden the currents of fertility that flow through the spring to become an important holiday in many Protestant churches, especially among African Americans. Reversing the harvest holiday of Thanksgiving, when people stay home and most restaurants close, the celebration of motherhood in spring creates the busiest restaurant scene of the year.

The strongest bonds of many people to Christianity or to Judaism have nothing to do with beliefs about resurrection or exodus from Egypt, but with the pagan practices associated with holidays. Rabbits lay no eggs, and neither rabbits nor eggs have anything to do with the Jesus of the Christian Scriptures; but rabbits and eggs both mean fertility, the aspect of nature that people enjoy celebrating in spring. At Passover, fertility appears in the egg on the Seder plate, as well as in the salt water (of the womb) in which the herbs are dipped, and in the story of the holiday, which includes killing a lamb to save the other firstborn.

Judaism resists seasonal rites, with their connections to myth, and insists upon history more than Christianity does, but the realm of myth also claims Jews. At Christmas and Hanukkah and at Easter and Passover, Judaism and Christianity resemble denominations more and more and separate religions less. The power of the seasons gradually displaces history.

New Year's Day serves as a secular exit from our sacred time.

Rabbits and eggs

both mean fertility,

the aspect of nature that

people enjoy celebrating

in spring.

Such displacement accelerates when the domestic activities of a holiday outweigh formal and public activities, and when leadership of the celebration passes from clergy to laity.

The same mythological transformation that befalls holidays of the historical faiths can also affect civil observances. On Memorial Day, the seasonal power of domestic religion has largely overcome history. What began as a day of reconciliation after the Civil War gradually became, through the grim struggles of the twentieth century, a solemn remembrance of those who fought all foreign enemies in the name of freedom for the people of the United States. But now, late in the 1990s, the day proclaims the beginning of summer. Beaches open on the northeastern coasts; people have their first outdoor barbecues and get their first sunburns. Though parades still take place, music teachers no longer demand that our children march in step. Brownie troops, Little League teams, and students of commercial karate schools walk up Main Street in their uniforms and costumes. In many towns, the army jeeps and trucks of decades past have disappeared, and the ranks of veterans willing and able to march have thinned to the point of vanishing. The barbecue has become the sacrament.

Throughout our calendar, the seasonal aspect of holidays—whether it was original as with Christmas or secondary as with Memorial Day—gradually displaces history. The Fourth of July, fixed on that day rather than a Monday because of historic fact, now serves with Memorial Day as the bracket of high summer; together, Memorial Day and July 4 surround the moment of the summer solstice that the Druids celebrated at Stonehenge. The fireworks of the Fourth have a glorious, but melancholy aspect—already the days grow shorter, and they will do so until Christmas. Labor Day, the last party of the summer, sees few parades and little acknowledgment of labor unions these days; it has become a substitute for Lammas, the pagan feast of the first grain harvest that falls on August 1.

Nowhere does the pagan influence on our domestic religion appear so strongly as on October 31, Halloween, the former Samhain, the day of the dead that marks the midway point between the sun's decline after the autumn equinox and the sun's death in winter. Once Halloween in the United States belonged to Irish immigrants whose Catholic practice had not obliterated their connections with the pagan Celts. By the midtwentieth century, it was a children's holiday accepted by most people in this country; but in the 1980s and '90s, Halloween has become a big event on college campuses and a day for costume parades inside the public schools. We now spend more money celebrating Halloween than on any holiday other than Christmas.

Evangelical Christians protest, since Halloween clearly comes from the pagan calendar and leads people to dress their children as demons. When Catholics baptized what the Druids called Samhain as All Saints' Day, which the Roman church still celebrates on November 1, the idea of a more general contact between the living and all the dead turned intensely negative. The night before All Saints'—All Hallows' Eve, or Halloween—became a time exclusively for the non-sainted dead, the restless and the damned. Although the Catholic calendar celebrates All Souls' Day on November 2, a day of prayer for all the dead not known to be saints, the damned will have their due. The growing power of Halloween and the attempts of some churches to bring it inside may eventually produce an autumn version of the universal Ancestors' Day that Shinto provides for Japan, that Memorial Day briefly was, and that our domestic religion needs.

Within Islam, because it fiercely resists idols and because its lunar calendar means that the fast of Ramadan, the holy month of pilgrimage, and the two *eid* holidays travel through the solar year, believers often make serious attempts to keep themselves and their children free from the seasonal forces of our domestic religion. But Muslims who live far from the equator know the variations of sunrise and sunset by the timing of their daily prayers, the content of which follows not the seasons but the sections of the Qur'an; and even Muslims in the United States have to take Christmas breaks from school. Muslims often participate in the opening of the midwinter holiday at Thanksgiving and watch the last moment of the holiday's closing on Super Bowl Sunday in January. For all groups the domestic religion makes mythic time, or cyclical time, inexorably more important as opposed to historical, linear time.

The seasonal power of domestic religion has largely overcome history.

Culture has reached

an impasse from which all

of history looks equally

relevant and irrelevant.

Our increasingly seasonal holidays testify that U.S. culture has reached an impasse from which all of history looks equally relevant and irrelevant. Emma Goldman and Thomas Jefferson, Martin Luther King, Abraham Lincoln, W. E .B. DuBois, and Malcolm X seem equally contemporary. In our educational practice, we try to teach students to see patterns of similarity and difference between such people, and we downplay lists of dates and events. Meanwhile, perhaps in an attempt to repair the loss of history, studies of the life cycle and the stages of development from childhood through adulthood hold more and more interest. People seek norms and standards and practical advice from stage theories, where once they hoped for solutions through behavioral manipulation, drugs, or psychoanalysis. Sometimes it seems that we naively think that recognizing patterns can prevent difficulties, as though understanding Carl Jung's analysis of obsession with anima and animus figures could inoculate people against their midlife crises.

Seen in historical perspective, the discovery and definition of life stages themselves reveal as much social construction as biological determination. When three-year-olds fed chickens and six-year-olds milked cows, the culture recognized infancy but not childhood; the Bible speaks very little of children as a separate category of people. Social history since Philippe Aries documents the emergence of Western consciousness of the child as an event of the late eighteenth and early nineteenth centuries, roughly contemporary with Romanticism and the Industrial Revolution.[5] From the 1880s through the 1930s, with the work of Sigmund Freud, G. Stanley Hall, and Erik Erikson, adolescence came into its own. As culture absorbed Jung in the 1950s and '60s, the issues of meaning in middle age gained recognition; and the elderly arrived in the work of Robert Butler in the '70s. Reporter Gail Sheehy popularized developmental stages in her 1980s bestseller, *Passages;* now she follows the baby boom with *The Silent Passage,* a book on menopause. Today, people evaluate their own lives and those of others with many concepts, such as the identity crisis and the midlife crisis, regression and repressed memory, developmental delays and reminiscence for life review, which did not exist before this century.

Even with all these tools, however, within the domestic religion the power of seasons resists history. The concept of a self that remains the same, traveling through time as a ship goes through weather, tends to absorb and defeat developmental perspectives, whatever truth they may hold. Sometimes it seems that astrology, reincarnation, or some theory of the return of ancestors must be programmed into us as the default position for our concept of human lifetimes.

Integrity—the coherence and wholeness of a single life, quite apart from the standards of church or state and contributions to the world—has become a primary value, perhaps the only value that our domestic religion professes to hold higher than success. Although Erikson named integrity the virtue of the last stage of life,[6] integrity has a timeless quality, and the sense of timelessness grows because so many therapies and theories involve recalling the past and projecting the future. When people in their fifties think of themselves parenting an "inner child" and adults spend hundreds of dollars on Halloween costumes for themselves and Christmas gifts for other adults, while Disney World promotes itself as a resort for adults without children and Las Vegas develops into a Disney World for adults, we approach an ideal or a fantasy in which all the stages of life are present at once. Investigations of genealogy extend the definition of integrity across generations. With past-life therapy, Scientology, and the channeling of collective entities, ever more elaborate manipulations of development seek to liberate all of time in the present moment.

Behind this collapse of past and future into the present lurks a troubling but also exciting truth about our position in history. We live not only at the artificial turn of a millennium—attributing inordinate meaning to round numbers and forgetting the narrowly Christian and historically incorrect measurement of these millennia—we also stand at the real end of an era, with no sense of direction. Outsiders as different as Francis Fukuyama, who wrote a seminal but often-ridiculed article on "The End of History" in 1989, and James Redfield, whose novel *The Celestine Prophecy* spent four years in the mid-1990s on the hardcover bestseller list while being ignored by intellectuals,

> Ever more elaborate manipulations of development seek to liberate all of time in the present moment.

The momentum that began with the Renaissance and Reformation has played itself out.

testify to the same sense of a pause or historic plateau, as do all of the artists and critics who call themselves postmodern. The momentum that began with the Renaissance and Reformation and that carried the West through the Enlightenment, romanticism, the Victorian era, and modernism has played itself out. Not only do young people not know the difference between Lutherans and Presbyterians, they know enough not to care.

Where an increasing empire of Western thinking seemed inevitable to everyone in the 1930s, no one now entertains such expectations. Sixty years ago, many college students sensibly assumed that the whole world would soon be Christian. After all, Madame Chiang Kai-shek, the first lady of China, was a Methodist educated at Wellesley, and most of the business and government elite of Korea was Presbyterian. Westerners believed in the great favors Britain was doing India and associated Hinduism with primitive practices, like the caste system and the custom of a widow immolating herself on her husband's funeral pyre. Christians in Lebanon and Syria worked to convert Muslims. People dismissed Buddhism as fatalistic pessimism and as a willing handmaid of the Japanese empire.

The aftermath of the Second World War brought some of these colonial attitudes to an end, but U.S. Peace Corps missionaries and Special Forces counterinsurgency teams proved that we still thought we should tell the world how to live. Even in the early 1970s, college students studied the Reformation and the rise of the middle class in course after course, whether they took English literature or political science, sociology or religious studies, not to mention history itself. Those attracted to Marx simply followed a more radical variant of the same plot.

About 1975, with the fall of Saigon and the oil embargoes, our master story of Western progress weakened; the critiques of African Americans, feminists, Western ethnics, and non-Western peoples have since consigned the story itself to history. A narrative of the modern West no longer has any privileged place in college curricula, or any place at all in the liberal arts programs of many students. Rage at the loss of this story powers the backlash against multiculturalism among commentators like George Will and Pat Buchanan; bafflement in a world without a controlling narrative leads many to follow fundamentalists of all kinds. In place of what historian William McNeill called *The Rise of the West,* we have no integrated story of world history.

On the positive side, we do see some facts more clearly without the old narrative. Until ten years ago, the aims of German and especially of Japanese leaders in World War II remained opaque to me, despite fifteen years of higher education. Raised with a "madman theory" regarding Hitler and Pearl Harbor, I thought simply that the United States had won a great war for democracy against nations who wanted, against all probability of success, to conquer and to enslave the world. Contact with Pakistanis, Indians, and Africans has since given me another perspective: that the war began as a desperate grab by industrial nations that had lost in the scramble for colonies against the nations that had won. I began to consider such anomalies as the Dutch ruling Indonesia, which is now the fourth most populous nation in the world, and to appreciate that the British Empire was the largest, richest, and most powerful empire the world has ever known. I noticed that in 1931, when Japan invaded Manchuria, Japan was the only entirely independent country in all of Asia and Africa. Suddenly, as I imagined Japanese leaders contemplating the British in India and Hong Kong and Shanghai and Singapore, the French in Indochina, and the Americans in the Philippines, the Japanese colonization of Korea and Manchuria and the attack on Pearl Harbor made sense.

Without an identity linked to a group, the rituals and values of daily life that compose domestic religion hold life together less effectively. The Japanese and Germans lost the war and have engaged ever since in a long struggle with their identities; as victor, the United States emerged from the war secure and took up a crusade against communism that kept our identity fixed. But now, people on every street in the United States identify first with Africa and Asia, with nations of Native Americans and with various Western religious and ethnic groups, and only then with the United States. These multiple identities do not necessarily lead to ingratitude or to disloyalty; people whom Theodore Roosevelt would have scorned as "hy-

We do see some facts

more clearly without the

old narrative.

> The ancestors nourished the living family, and to protect their land one might well fight or die.

phenated Americans" and dragged to the melting pot have proven willing to die for this country. Statements that the United States is "the greatest nation on earth" still come from both liberal and conservative politicians; yet agreement on the meaning and even on the relevant facts of our story has receded to the vanishing point.

Narratives need to connect time with place as well as with group. About ninety years ago in Italy, my late father's first job as a child of seven was to throw old bones back into new graves. Because his village of Roccatagliata, in the mountains near Genoa, used its graveyard over and over, starting again at one corner when they ran out of space, every funeral disturbed the bones of centuries past. Fustel de Coulanges, the pioneer anthropologist who wrote *The Ancient City,* found the essence of patriotism—social continuity and group identity extended over time—in cemeteries. As Coulanges saw it, to ancient Romans the *patria* meant literally the "fatherland," the ground where the fathers lay buried. To that power sacrifice was made; libations were poured to continue the link.[7] The ancestors nourished the living family, and to protect their land one might well fight or die. Near the front door of the church at Roccatagliata is a plaque commemorating the dead of World War II; the plaque lists about two dozen names, and all of them are Gardellas. The goal of becoming an honored ancestor for a particular people has brought a sense of completion to the life cycle for most adults throughout history.

But when people move four or five times in their lives, sometimes alone and sometimes with spouses and children, what power remains in cemeteries or in history? Who will return in a hundred years to pray, to read the headstones, or even to dig up the grave to add new family members to the communion of the dead? The last thirty years have seen a radical decline in the visitation of graves on Memorial Day (which was once called Decoration Day, because people brought flags, flowers, and other decorations to the cemeteries). The last seventy years have seen Catholics cease to have wakes in their homes, transforming the tradition of a final meal, party, and vigil with the deceased into an hour or two of formal reception in a funeral home. Such detachment from the dead of our own families may seem unfortunate, but it also opens a way for the domestic religion to develop a sense of communion with all the dead. Then perhaps even monotheists, for all their allegiance to a God who acts in history, could find something of the joyful reverence for the cycle of life on earth that they now envy in the traditional, "pagan" religions of indigenous peoples.

According to King Adefunmi I, who serves as monarch of the African American Yoruba community that has thrived for the last thirty years at Oyotunji, South Carolina, Yoruba religion is not faith but practice. True religion means not contact with God, the general power that gives life but has no plans, but harmony with ancestors who give us laws and customs. At the Parliament of the World's Religions in Chicago in 1993, I heard Adefunmi argue that most of the religious insanity and extremism in the world results from people failing to connect with the spirits of their own ancestors and identifying instead with someone else's. He used the example of Minister Louis Farrakhan of the Nation of Islam to exemplify those who, in his opinion, chose the wrong spiritual guides; he said that Farrakhan became unbalanced because he followed the Arab prophet Muhammad rather than the gods and ancestors of West Africa. When the audience asked Adefunmi what guides we in the United States should follow, since almost everyone here lives far from ancestral cemeteries and sometimes with uncertainty about their lineage, he answered that all people should follow their own ancestors, using mediums to find them if necessary, but they should also get "in touch with the landlords" of the place where they live. We should honor those who lived on the land before us, Adefunmi taught, because the power of their spirits forms part of the system of nature that supports everything in being.

Visions of the United States as a sacred land, and even attempts to seek peace with the dead natives of the land (many of whom we whites killed), have gone on for centuries, but they reached a rhetorical climax in the administration of Ronald Reagan. Often referring to the United States as a land God set "between two great oceans" so that "a people who love freedom" could find sanctuary there, Reagan ended his last public address as president by collapsing time, history, and place

Reagan's farewell address showed how the domestic religion can swallow symbols from the civil religion.

A land where

Pilgrims and Indians,

Europeans and Africans

and Asians all become

honored ancestors.

into a single eternal image: the city on a hill. Domestic both in medium—this was a television speech with no public audience, direct from President Reagan's home to millions of other private homes—and in the message of domestic happiness, Reagan's farewell address showed how the domestic religion can swallow symbols from the civil religion and make those symbols its own.

When John Winthrop, governor of the Massachusetts Bay Colony, first called this nation a "city on a hill," he spoke to a stockholders' meeting, a meeting of the Massachusetts Bay Company, aboard the ship *Arbella* in what would become Boston Harbor. Not only did Winthrop give a public discourse; his purpose was also public. He quoted Matthew 5:14, in the Sermon on the Mount, where Jesus tells his disciples to remember that the world will watch them. Winthrop hoped that Massachusetts would set an example for England and the world, so that all nations might adopt the forms of religion and government that his Puritans would show them.

But for Reagan (in the words of speechwriter Peggy Noonan), the U.S. city on a hill served not as an example but as the destination of the saved, drawn from all humanity and drawing together all history. "How stands the city on this night?" Reagan asked. He pictured it "standing tall on [its] granite ridge, wind swept, God blessed," with walls that had gates that were always open to those with the faith and heart to reach it. Its streets teemed with commerce, and its beacon held steady to guide all the pilgrims "hurtling through the darkness toward home." Reagan's vision came not from Matthew 5 or John Winthrop, despite his citation of the governor, but from Revelation 21, where John of Patmos described New Jerusalem, the apocalyptic City of God, whose streets also filled with riches and whose gates stood always open, an island of light in the darkness. In turn, New Jerusalem descended from the new Temple and city in Ezekiel 40–48. A goal that lay beyond the historic future for Ezekiel and for John became for Reagan an eternally present reality. To millions of U.S. homes, the farewell speech brought images implying that we already live in the New Jerusalem.

Does this identification of the United States with the City of God represent idolatry, or can it lead beyond itself? Robert Bellah asked a similar question about U.S. civil religion, and he prescribed expansion as the cure: a worldwide civil religion, based on reverence for documents like the United Nations Universal Declaration of Human Rights. But in the domestic religion, the way to escape idolatry moves inward rather than outward, from the general to the specific—from a land set aside for freedom to a land where Pilgrims and Indians, Europeans and Africans and Asians all become honored ancestors. Their descendants could then try to share with each other and to live with the earth to keep the rest of the world in balance. Seasons and history, natural and biblical traditions may be moving toward such harmony in the domestic religion today.

Columnist Ben Wattenberg has called the United States "the first universal nation," and some of us are no doubt trying to write a new universal version of world history. While working, often contentiously, on the drafts of such a story, modern Americans may be learning how to live in a present suffused by past and future. The truth about time seems to appear more and more in cycles, in spirals, and in multiple, conflicting narratives.

· II · BEYOND RELIGIONS

Beyond the round of seasons, stages of life, and eras of history lies death. Fear of death explains much of our chronic interest in the end of the world: if the whole world ends, then life will not go on without me and I will not die alone. When considering death from a distance, people may find comfort in having lived a successful life; but imminent death can destroy such comforts, and death finally conquers both successful people and failures. The rituals of formal religions, refined over millennia, face their most severe test, and often fail and look feeble and empty, in handling death. What chance do the rituals and values of domestic religion have?

This book has taken the domestic religion of the United States as a phenomenon, the result of a mixture of many religious traditions under certain social conditions, a fact of life to be described and analyzed. To complete the description, some predictions of development have been made, and these have led in turn to prescriptions for dealing with some of the difficulties imposed by the rituals and values of everyday life. Now the moment has come to face more basic questions. Do human beings need to have religions at all? Do religions connect us to any sources of value, any happiness or fulfillment, beyond the rewards and punishments that those who follow the religions provide for each other?

Evangelical Christians frequently say that religion cannot save anyone. You may go to church, as revivalists have been preaching since Jonathan Edwards; you may think that you lead a moral life; but unless you know yourself as a sinner, confess your need for salvation, and ask Christ to save you, you die in your sins and sink into hell, forever excluded from the presence of God.

Horrible though this doctrine appears, it expresses this truth: religious people can be as vicious, prejudiced, selfish, and hateful as anyone on earth. In fact, orthodox religion itself, without any differentiation for type, may be one of the most predictive factors for sexual dysfunction, domestic violence, and what most would call biased views of race and gender.[1] Yet we turn to religion for comfort, for meaning, for reaffirmation of social bonds and basic values. As William James observed long ago, philosophy may be able with effort to maintain a good spirit in difficulty, but only religion has actually helped people to be happy while they suffer, "their souls growing in happiness just in proportion as their outward state grew more intolerable."[2] If religion itself is not entirely good or sufficient to the needs of life, then perhaps religion prepares people for another step that leads to the strength James describes. The nature of that step appears by implication in the etymology of the word *religion*. The Latin *ligare*, "to bind," the same root as ligament, and the prefix indicating "repetition" make up the word. Religion binds, or rebinds that which has come apart. As I defined it in the first chapter, a religion is a system of nonrational commitments that holds life together.

But no life holds together for long. Again to quote James, "The sanest and best of us are of one clay with lunatics and prison inmates, and death finally runs the robustest of us down."[3] Religion fulfills its most important role by making us feel secure enough to let go, to release ourselves and others from the commitments, rituals, and values of religion itself. If religion has helped us to realize what values we live by and what we would die for, to know the standards we use to judge ourselves, then we can learn to stop judging, to live and to let others live, to accept that even if there is nothing to die for, still we must die. Only such absolute trust, usually called faith, keeps religious systems from becoming deadly constraints of all thought and sympathy.

Fear of death explains much of our chronic interest in the end of the world.

In personal relations, to let go with absolute trust is to love. Religion can enshrine love, but no religion can create it; like faith, love transcends all specific values and rituals. Religion affects where love is expressed, not what love is.

The English language has often been criticized for applying the single word *love* to parents and children, husbands and wives, friends, animals, and to the relations of people to their favorite foods. In contrast, some Christians point out that two Greek terms in the Christian Scriptures appear in English as "love": the *philia* of friends and the *agape* that believers share among themselves and with God. Such writers may also mention that Greek has a third term, *eros,* for sexual love. Yet there is an undeniable strength in having one word for this attitude of trust, these caring actions, this gaze of unconditional attention and regard. By calling every relation from parent and child to diner and food by the name of love, we emphasize the unity of human nature. The biblical picture of humanity—not to mention the Aristotelian doctrine of rational souls, the Taoist view of nature, or the nondualist metaphysics of Hindus and Buddhists—does not drive wedges between body and mind or heart and brain, but sees the whole person together as the subject and object of love.

When trust extends to everyone and everything without distinction, love becomes compassion. Compassion does not choose anyone positively, as love does, but accepts everyone who comes. When Buddhists paint compassion they use moonlight, because the moon shines on all things gently, without heat. Sentiments, special feelings of attachment to one person or one object, limit compassion by heightening awareness in some directions, for example, toward those people who share feelings with us or those objects we have long known. The light of compassion falls equally on the alien, the repellent, and the strange. Like faith and love, compassion transcends religion; compassionate people let go of their religions and extend attention even to those who violate their values.

The values beyond religion come together in awareness, which may be the best word available at the moment for unqualified good. In awareness of pain, the pain is bad, but the awareness is good; medicine seeks to relieve suffering without eliminating or clouding awareness. If the Gospel of John rightly says that the Word is God and that God is the Word, then God is active awareness, expressing itself without distinction of subject and object. Modern scientists seeking the link between quantum physics and consciousness also seek this absolute.

According to the most ancient Hindu poems, the Vedas, the original Spirit or Purusha of a thousand eyes, who is all that has been and all that is to be, can be called the God of "immortality which waxes greater still by food."[4] In other words, sacrifice paradoxically contributes to the strength of divinity. Awareness increases because of faith, love, and compassion and gives them strength in return.

Awareness always transcends religious practice, although that transcendence can be described both positively and negatively. From the positive side, awareness works as the keystone of an arch, in which the walls are the commitments and values of religion. Here the rituals of religion act in the way that Aristotle said that good health habits and moral virtues act, building up the soul for the higher, intellectual virtues, the highest of which is wisdom, the capacity to contemplate the truth (another name for awareness).[5] Following Aristotle, spiritual teachers of the West have taught that religion should prepare people for the contemplation of truth, the highest purpose and greatest happiness of the rational soul, and the action in which humanity most closely approaches God.

On the negative side, our attachment to religion, to moral virtues, and even to good health may distract us from the absolute truth to which awareness points: that the whole realm of matter and measurable phenomena depends on an invisible, infinite realm in which we are always, at every moment, free to will the good. The metaphor of arch and keystone, higher and lower virtues misleads, because only the presence or absence of awareness makes the most trivial ritual or the grandest moral action worthwhile or empty. This approach finds support in the philosophy of Immanuel Kant, and its most characteristic practitioners among Protestants and Zen Buddhists.[6]

Hesitating between two truths, it may be comforting to reflect that we actually have no choice. We live on what Hindus and Buddhists would call the sea of samsara, composed of

Like faith and love, compassion transcends religion.

desires and ignorance, yielding a chaos of karma and reincarnations. From the Jewish and Christian perspective, we might say that the world still floats on the abyss over which the Spirit of God hovers, commanding the sea to keep to its boundaries. The rituals and values of our lives are like so many boats or islands on that sea, passed to us by parents and teachers at the end of an immemorial chain of transmission. Some of these rituals may well go back to whatever common ancestors we share with chimpanzees, who can still be seen dancing in circles and shaking their heads back and forth during thunderstorms.

Whether we decide to try to build rationally on the religions we find or to cultivate an attitude of detachment from them is a practical, social judgment about how well religions serve our best good in particular situations. Whatever conclusions we reach, studying the patterns of religion with a good will should increase our awareness, compassion, love, and even faith.

NOTES

1. FROM RELIGION TO DOMESTIC RELIGION

1. Charlton T. Lewis and Charles Short, *A Latin Dictionary* (1879; Oxford: Clarendon Press, 1969), 1556.

2. William James, *The Varieties of Religious Experience* (1902; New York: Longmans, Green and Company, 1920), 50.

3. Robert Bellah, "Civil Religion in America," *Daedalus* 96 (1967): 1-21; Colleen McDannell, *The Christian Home in Victorian America, 1840–1900* (Bloomington: Indiana University Press, 1986), 150–51; David D. Hall, ed., *Lived Religion in America: Toward a History of Practice* (Princeton: Princeton University Press, 1997).

4. Emile Durkheim, *The Division of Labor in Society,* trans. George Simpson (New York: Macmillan, 1933), actually makes this case more cogently than his more frequently cited *Elementary Forms of Religious Life;* Alan Wolfe, *One Nation, After All* (New York: Viking, 1998), 62; Diana Eck, "The Mosque Next Door," *Harvard Magazine,* September–October 1996; also see Diana Eck, "Challenge of Pluralism," *Nieman Reports* 47, no. 2 (summer 1993).

5. Durkheim, *The Division of Labor in Society,* 172.

6. For further exploration, try Joseph Campbell, *The Hero with a Thousand Faces;* Carl Jung, *Modern Man in Search of a Soul;* Mircea Eliade, *The Sacred and the Profane;* Rudolf Otto, *The Idea of the Holy.*

7. For further detail about this transformation, try Ramsay MacMullen, *Constantine* (New York: Dial Press, 1969); John Gager, *Kingdom and Community* (Englewood Cliffs, N.J.: Prentice-Hall, 1975); Wayne Meeks, *The First Urban Christians* (New Haven, Conn.: Yale University Press, 1983); Robin Lane Fox, *Pagans and Christians* (London: Viking, 1986); and Wayne Meeks, *The Origins of Christian Morality* (New Haven, Conn.: Yale University Press, 1993).

2. SUCCESS

1. My information on the value of talents of silver comes from Elwyn E. Tilden and Bruce M. Metzger, note to Matthew 25:15 in *The New Oxford Annotated Bible* (New York: Oxford University Press, 1991).

2. Frederick Mathewson Denny, *An Introduction to Islam* (New York: Macmillan, 1994), 120, 388.

3. An accessible discussion of these doctrines can be found in the chapter on Buddhism in Huston Smith, *The World's Religions,* which many libraries own under its earlier title, *The Religions of Man.* For further detail, see John Snelling, *The Buddhist Handbook* (Rochester, Vt.: Inner Traditions International, 1991).

4. Lao Tzu, *Tao Te Ching*, trans. D. C. Lau (New York: Penguin Books, 1963), 75, 96 (Book 1, chapters 19 and 37).

5. Max Weber, *The Protestant Ethic and the Spirit of Capitalism*, trans. Talcott Parsons (1930; reprint, London: Routledge, 1992).

3. WORK

1. Weber, *The Protestant Ethic and the Spirit of Capitalism*, 35.

2. Ibid., 59–60.

3. Wade Clark Roof and William McKinney, *American Mainline Religion* (Englewood Cliffs, N.J.: Prentice-Hall, 1987); Andrew Greeley has been following this pattern of achievement in many publications; see especially *The Catholic Myth* (New York: Charles Scribner's Sons, 1990), 73–76, and *Religious Change in America* (Cambridge: Harvard University Press, 1989), 76–86.

4. Karl Marx, from *The German Ideology*, A2; my text from Jon Elster, ed., *Karl Marx: A Reader* (New York: Cambridge University Press, 1986).

5. Shunryu Suzuki, *Zen Mind, Beginner's Mind*, touches the subject, as do all basic instruction books in Buddhist practice. For a richer reflection, see Shundo Aoyama, *Zen Seeds: Reflections of a Female Priest* (1983; Tokyo: Kosei Publishing Company, 1990), 86–98.

6. Lao Tzu, *Tao Te Ching*, 140 (chapter 78).

7. For this point I am indebted to Bill Duesing, an environmental activist who broadcasts weekly on public radio station WSHU in Bridgeport, Connecticut.

8. Karl Marx and Friedrich Engels, "The Communist Manifesto," in *Capital and Other Writings* (New York: The Modern Library, 1959), 333. In other editions of the manifesto, this passage occurs in the next-to-the-last paragraph of part 1.

4. FOOD

1. Claude Lévi-Strauss, *The Raw and the Cooked: Introduction to a Science of Mythology*, trans. John and Doreen Weightman (1964; New York: Harper & Row, 1969), 143, 339. Lévi-Strauss first advanced his complete culinary triangle in *L'Arc* 26: 19–29; an English translation appeared in *Partisan Review* 33 (1966): 586–95. A discussion of the development of this classification of cooling operations and its later modifications appears in Jack Goody, *Cooking, Cuisine, and Class* (Cambridge: Cambridge University Press, 1982), 17–29, 216–20.

2. See Gerald Carson, *Cornflake Crusade* (New York: Rinehart and Co., 1957).

3. Frederick J. Simmons, *Food in China* (Boca Raton, Fla.: CRC Press, 1991), 23, 31–36.

4. Isaac Bashevis Singer, *Enemies: A Love Story* (1972; New York: Farrar, Straus and Giroux, 1992), 257.

5. Peter Gardella, *Innocent Ecstasy: How Christianity Gave America an Ethic of Sexual Pleasure* (New York: Oxford University Press, 1985), 44–49.

6. James Redfield, *The Celestine Prophecy* (New York: Warner Books, 1993), 51.

5. SPORTS

1. Rolfe Humphries, "Polo Grounds," in Charles Einstein, ed., *The Fireside Book of Baseball* (New York: Simon and Schuster, 1956), 205.

2. Carl G. Jung, "Transformation Symbolism in the Mass" (1941), section II, part 4. Reprinted in C. G. Jung, *Psyche and Symbol: A Selection from the Writings of C. G. Jung*, ed. Violet S. de Laszlo (Garden City, N.Y.: Doubleday Anchor Books, 1958), 158. Also,

see C. G. Jung, "Dream Symbolism in Relation to Alchemy," in *The Portable Jung,* ed. Joseph Campbell (New York: Viking, 1976), 381.

3. Carl G. Jung, "A Psychological Approach to the Dogma of the Trinity," in *Psychology and Religion: West and East,* vol. 11 of *The Collected Works of Carl G. Jung,* trans. R. F. C. Hull (Princeton, N.J.: Princeton University Press, 1973).

4. Martin Buber, *I and Thou,* trans. Walter Kaufmann (1937; New York: Charles Scribner's Sons, 1970), 59.

5. Michael Novak, *The Joy of Sports* (New York: Basic Books, 1976), 101.

6. Jim Dwyer, "Sweetheart Deal? Scan Yanks' Tab," New York *Daily News,* Aug. 26, 1997, 4.

7. Alison Futrell, *Blood in the Arena* (Austin: University of Texas Press, 1998), 48–51.

6. ENTERTAINMENT

1. Phyllis A. Tickle, *God-Talk in America* (New York: Crossroad, 1997), 15.

2. Jung, *The Portable Jung,* ed. Campbell, 45. Selection from "The Structure and Dynamics of the Psyche," in Jung, *Collected Works,* vol. 8.

3. Durkheim, *The Division of Labor in Society,* 79.

4. Henry Adams, *Mont St.-Michel and Chartres* (1904; Marietta, Ga.: Larlin Corporation, 1982), 104. Adams explored the religion of world's fairs further in his autobiography, *The Education of Henry Adams* (Boston: Houghton Mifflin, 1918), 339, 379.

5. Wendy Doniger O'Flaherty, *Other People's Myths* (New York: Macmillan, 1988), 39.

6. Immanuel Kant's essay, "Perpetual Peace," which proposed a disarmed community of prosperous nations, formed part of the subject of Henry Kissinger's undergraduate honors essay at Harvard. For Gingrich and the Tofflers, see Alvin and Heidi Toffler, *Creating a New Civilization* (Atlanta: Turner Publishing, 1994).

7. Francis Fukuyama, *The End of History and the Last Man* (New York: The Free Press, 1992). Fukuyama's first article, "The End of History?" appeared in *The National Interest* in the summer of 1989.

8. Frank Tipler, *The Physics of Immortality* (New York: Doubleday, 1994), 157.

7. DRINK, DRUGS, AND SOBRIETY

1. Translation of the *Masabih as-Sunna* in Arthur Jeffrey, *Islam* (New York: Liberal Arts Press, 1958); excerpted in Mircea Eliade, ed., *Essential Sacred Writings from Around the World* (San Francisco: HarperSanFrancisco, 1977), 516–17.

2. James, *The Varieties of Religious Experience,* 387.

3. Ibid.

4. Ibid.

5. Ibid., 389.

6. William Johnston, *Silent Music: The Science of Meditation* (1974; San Francisco: Harper & Row, 1979), 34.

7. Kathleen Norris, *The Cloister Walk* (1996; New York: Riverhead, 1997), 170–72.

8. Associated Press, "Clare Booth Luce Took LSD 'Trips'," *The New Haven Register,* Oct. 23, 1997, A15.

9. Peter McDermott, Alan Matthews, Pat O'Hare, and Andrew Bennett, "Ecstasy in the United Kingdom: Recreational Drug Use and Subcultural Change," in Nick Heather, Alex Wodak, Ethan A. Nadelmann, and Pat O'Hare, eds., *Psychoactive Drugs and Harm Reduction: From Faith to Science* (London: Whurr Publishers, 1993), 230–44.

8. SEX, LOVE, AND FRIENDSHIP

1. Vic Ziegel, "Yanks Tossin' and Turnin'," New York *Daily News,* Oct. 8, 1997, 58.

2. Ed Wheat, M.D., and Gaye Wheat, *Intended for Pleasure* (1977; Old Tappan, N.J.: Fleming H. Revell, 1981), 83. The same advice was given by a minister in Tim and Beverly La Haye, *The Act of Marriage* (Grand Rapids, Mich.: Zondervan, 1976).

3. Alfred C. Kinsey et al., *Sexual Behavior in the Human Female* (New York: Pocket Books, 1953, 1973), 298–99, 380, 403.

4. Francis Wayland, *The Elements of Moral Science* (1837; Cambridge: Harvard University Press, 1963), 270. On this phase of Sanger's education, see Gardella, *Innocent Ecstasy,* 131–32.

5. Adolphe Tanquerey, *The Spiritual Life* (Paris: Desclee, 1930), is a text used by Roman Catholic seminaries in the United States for much of the twentieth century.

6. The clearest reporting of the work of Masters and Johnson appeared in Mary Jane Sherfey, *The Nature and Evolution of Female Sexuality* (New York: Random House, 1972), 109–10. For critiques of their work, see Barbara Ehrenreich, *Re-Making Love* (Garden City, N.Y.: Doubleday, 1986). For the original, see William H. Masters and Virginia E. Johnson, *Human Sexual Response* (Boston: Little, Brown, 1966).

7. Shere Hite, *The Hite Report* (1976; New York: Dell, 1977), 59.

8. Anthony Kosnik et al., *Human Sexuality* (New York: Paulist Press, 1978).

9. Peter W. Williams, *Popular Religion in America* (Englewood Cliffs, N.J.: Prentice-Hall, 1980), 212–14.

10. See Jonathan Ned Katz, *The Invention of Heterosexuality* (New York: Penguin, 1995.)

11. Joseph Campbell, *The Masks of God: Occidental Mythology* (1964; New York: Penguin, 1991), 504–17.

12. John Boswell, *Same-Sex Unions in Premodern Europe* (New York: Villard Books, 1994).

13. Michel Foucault, *The History of Sexuality,* vol. 1 (New York: Pantheon Books, 1978), 48.

9. EXERCISE, PRAYER, AND MAGIC

1. Surveys by the National Opinion Research Center, General Social Surveys, combined 1983 and 1984; reported in Richard John Neuhaus, ed., *Unsecular America* (Grand Rapids, Mich.: William B. Eerdmans, 1986), 140.

2. James F. Fixx, *The Complete Book of Running* (New York: Random House, 1977), xxi, 15.

3. Louis J. Puhl, S.J., ed. and trans., *The Spiritual Exercises of St. Ignatius* (Chicago: Loyola University Press, 1951), 2, 12, 25–28. In other editions, see the first exercise for the first week.

4. Artistotle, *Ethics,* trans. J. A. K. Thompson (1953; New York: Penguin, 1979), 109 (1109a25–b15).

5. F. C. Happold, *Mysticism* (1963; New York: Penguin, 1970), 56–100, provides a good brief discussion of the succession of purgation, illumination, and union; in an anthology section of the book, Happold also provides examples from ancient to modern times. Benedict Groeschel organized his *Spiritual Passages* (New York: Crossroad, 1989) according to these stages, as did Evelyn Underhill in her classic *Mysticism* (Oxford: Oneworld Publications, 1994).

6. Carl Jung, "Answer to Job," reprinted in Campbell, ed., *The Portable Jung,* 639–48 (chapter XIX, if you have *Answer to Job* in a separate edition). Jung also speculated on the connection between the Assumption of Mary and the acceptance of matter in 1948, before Pope Pius XII proclaimed that the Assumption was Catholic doctrine, in "A Psychological Approach to the Trinity," which appears in Jung, *Collected Works,* vol. 11, *Psychology and Religion: West and East,* 171.

7. Buber, *I and Thou,* 69, 122–55. In another translation, see the third part.

8. Meyer Levin, *Classic Hasidic Tales* (1932; New York: Penguin, 1975), 135–37. More examples of the earthly focus of Hasidic mysticism can be found in Dan Ben-Amos and Jerome R. Mintz, trans. and eds., *In Praise of the Baal Shem Tov* (Bloomington: Indiana University Press, 1970).

9. Buber, *I and Thou,* 57.

10. Keith Thomas, *Religion and the Decline of Magic* (New York: Charles Scribner's Sons, 1971), 656–57.

10. SEASONS

1. Mircea Eliade, *A History of Religious Ideas,* vol. 2 (Chicago: University of Chicago Press, 1982), 157.

2. Joan MacFarlane, "Kwanzaa Becoming Important to Retailers," December 27, 1995, http://cnnfn.com/archive/news/9512/27/kwanzaa/index.html.

3. Jung, *Modern Man in Search of a Soul,* 150–51.

4. Leigh Eric Schmidt, *Consumer Rites: The Buying and Selling of American Holidays* (Princeton: Princeton University Press, 1995), 246–56.

5. Philippe Aries, *Centuries of Childhood* (New York: Random House, 1965).

6. Erik Erikson, *Childhood and Society* (New York: W. W. Norton, 1950), 268–69, 273.

7. Numa Denis Fustel de Coulanges, *The Ancient City* (1864; Eng. trans. 1873; New York: Doubleday, 1956), 32, 39, 65, 89, 148.

11. BEYOND RELIGIONS

1. Martin Marty's study of fundamentalism, compiled with an enormous staff and published in several volumes as *Fundamentalisms Observed,* appears to confirm this view. Masters and Johnson in *Human Sexuality* also correlate orthodox belief with sexual dysfunction. William H. Masters, Virginia E. Johnson, and Robert C. Kolodny, *Human Sexuality,* 3d ed. (Glenview, Ill.: Scott, Foresman and Company, 1988), 510–11.

2. James, *The Varieties of Religious Experience,* 50.

3. Ibid., 47.

4. *Rig Veda,* X, 90, in Eliade, ed., *Essential Sacred Writings from Around the World,* 227.

5. This argument culminates in Aristotle's *Ethics,* trans. Thompson, Book Ten, and especially from sections 1175a10 to 1179b29.

6. The purest expressions that I know of how awareness transcends any preparation occur in the conclusion of Kant's *Groundwork for the Metaphysics of Morals* and in the sermon of Lin-chi, patriarch of Ch'an Buddhism, on the true monk who has left his home, which is translated in William Theodore de Bary, *The Buddhist Tradition* (New York: Modern Library, 1969), 225–31. See also Shunryu Suzuki, *Zen Mind, Beginner's Mind.*

SELECTED BIBLIOGRAPHY

Adams, Henry. *Mont St.-Michel and Chartres.* 1904. Marietta, Ga.: Larlin Corporation, 1982.

Aoyama, Shundo. *Zen Seeds: Reflections of a Female Priest.* Trans. Patricia Daien Bennage. 1983. Reprint, Tokyo: Kosei Publishing Company, 1990.

Bellah, Robert. "Civil Religion in America." *Daedalus* 96 (1967): 1–21.

Boswell, John. *Same-Sex Unions in Premodern Europe.* New York: Villard Books, 1994.

Brown, Karen McCarthy. *Mama Lola: A Voudou Priestess in Brooklyn.* Berkeley: University of California Press, 1991.

Buber, Martin. *I and Thou.* 1937. Trans. Walter Kaufmann. New York: Charles Scribner's Sons, 1970.

Campbell, Joseph. *The Hero with a Thousand Faces.* 1948. Princeton: Princeton University Press, 1968.

Carson, Gerald. *Cornflake Crusade.* New York: Rinehart and Co., 1957.

Denny, Frederick Mathewson. *An Introduction to Islam.* New York: Macmillan, 1994.

Durkheim, Emile. *The Division of Labor in Society.* 1893. Trans. George Simpson. New York: Macmillan, 1933.

Eck, Diana. *Encountering God.* Boston: Beacon Press, 1993.

Eliade, Mircea. *The Sacred and the Profane.* Trans. Willard R. Trask. New York: Harcourt, Brace & World, 1957.

Fixx, James F. *The Complete Book of Running.* New York: Random House, 1977.

Foucault, Michel. *The History of Sexuality, Volume I: An Introduction.* 1976. Trans. Robert Hurley. New York: Pantheon Books: 1978.

Fukuyama, Francis. *The End of History and the Last Man.* New York: The Free Press, 1992.

Fustel de Coulanges, Numa Denis. *The Ancient City.* 1864. New York: Doubleday, 1956.

Gardella, Peter. *Innocent Ecstasy: How Christianity Gave America an Ethic of Sexual Pleasure.* New York: Oxford University Press, 1985.

Goody, Jack. *Cooking, Cuisine, and Class.* Cambridge: Cambridge University Press, 1982.

Greeley, Andrew. *The Catholic Myth.* New York: Charles Scribner's Sons, 1990.

Hall, David D., ed. *Lived Religion in America: Toward a Theory of Practice.* Princeton: Princeton University Press, 1997.

Happold, F. C. *Mysticism.* 1963. New York: Penguin, 1970.

Heather, Nick, Alex Wodak, Ethan A. Nadelmann, and Pat O'Hare, eds. *Psychoactive Drugs and Harm Reduction: From Faith to Science.* London: Whurr Publishers, 1993.

Hite, Shere. *The Hite Report.* 1976. New York: Dell, 1977.

James, William. *The Varieties of Religious Experience.* 1902. London and New York: Longmans, Green and Co., 1920.

Johnston, William, 1974. *Silent Music: The Science of Meditation.* 1974. San Francisco: Harper & Row, 1976.

Jung, Carl G. *Modern Man in Search of a Soul.* Trans. W. S. Dell and Cary F. Baynes. New York: Harcourt Brace Jovanovich, 1933.

———. *Psyche and Symbol: A Selection from the Writings of C. G. Jung.* Ed. Violet S. de Laszlo. Garden City, N.Y.: Doubleday Anchor Books, 1958.

———. *Psychology and Religion: West and East.* Vol. 11 of *The Collected Works of Carl G. Jung.* Trans. R. F. C. Hull. 1969. Princeton, N.J.: Princeton University Press, 1973.

Katz, Jonathan Ned. *The Invention of Heterosexuality.* New York: Penguin, 1995.

Knaster, Mirka. *Discovering the Body's Wisdom.* New York: Bantam Books, 1996.

Kosnik, Anthony, et al. *Human Sexuality.* New York: Paulist Press, 1978.

Lao Tzu. *Tao Te Ching.* Trans. D.C. Lau. New York: Penguin Books, 1963.

Lenson, David. *On Drugs.* Minneapolis: University of Minnesota Press, 1995.

Lévi-Strauss, Claude. *The Raw and the Cooked. Introduction to a Science of Mythology.* 1964. Trans. John and Doreen Weightman. New York: Harper & Row, 1969.

McDannell, Colleen. *The Christian Home in Victorian America, 1840–1900.* Bloomington: Indiana University Press, 1986.

———. *Material Christianity.* New Haven, Conn.: Yale University Press, 1995.

Norris, Kathleen. *The Cloister Walk.* 1996. New York: Riverhead, 1997.

Novak, Michael. *The Joy of Sports.* New York: Basic Books, 1976.

O'Flaherty, Wendy Doniger. *Other People's Myths.* New York: Macmillan, 1988.

Redfield, James. *The Celestine Prophecy.* New York: Warner Books, 1993.

Roof, Wade Clark, and William McKinney. *American Mainline Religion.* Englewood Cliffs, N.J.: Prentice-Hall, 1987.

Schmidt, Leigh Eric. *Consumer Rites: The Buying and Selling of American Holidays.* Princeton: Princeton University Press, 1995.

Simon, Arthur. *Bread for the World.* 1975. New York: Paulist Press, 1984.

Singer, Isaac Bashevis. *Enemies: A Love Story.* 1972. New York: Farrar, Straus and Giroux, 1992.

Smith, Huston. *The World's Religions.* 1958. San Francisco: HarperSanFrancisco, 1991.

Snelling, John. *The Buddhist Handbook.* Rochester, Vt.: Inner Traditions International, 1991.

Suzuki, Shunryu. *Zen Mind, Beginner's Mind.* New York: Weatherhill, 1970.

Thomas, Keith. *Religion and the Decline of Magic.* New York: Charles Scribner's Sons, 1971.

Tickle, Phyllis A. *God-Talk in America.* New York: Crossroad, 1997.

Tilden, Elwyn E., and Bruce M. Metzger. *The New Oxford Annotated Bible.* New York: Oxford University Press, 1991.

Tipler, Frank. *The Physics of Immortality.* Garden City, N.Y.: Doubleday, 1994.

Toffler, Alvin and Heidi. *Creating a New Civilization.* Atlanta: Turner Publishing, 1994.

Wayland, Francis. *The Elements of Moral Science.* 1837. Cambridge, Mass.: Harvard University Press, 1963.

Weber, Max. *The Protestant Ethic and the Spirit of Capitalism.* 1904. Trans. Talcott Parsons. 1930. Reprint, London: Routledge, 1992.

Wheat, Ed, M.D., and Gaye Wheat. *Intended for Pleasure.* 1977. Old Tappan, N.J.: Fleming H. Revell, 1981.

Williams, Peter W. *Popular Religion in America.* Englewood Cliffs, N.J.: Prentice-Hall, 1980.

Wolfe, Alan. *One Nation, After All.* New York: Viking, 1998.